LA TABLE

LA RÂPE

LES CAROTTES

LE TABLIER

LE CONCOMBRE

LE CHOCOLAT

W9-APJ-785

LES VERRES

LES OEUFS

LE THYM

LA POMME

LES BADIANES

LE THERMOS

LE SOLEIL

LES PISTACHES

LES CRAYONS

LA CREVETTE

LES CORNICHONS

LES ASPERGES

LA CASSEROLE

LE COUTEAU

L'OIGNON

LES TOMATES CERISE

LE CHOU

UNE COUPE DE CHAMPAGNE

LES RAISINS

LA LIMONADE

LE BEURRE

LE BLANC D'ŒUF
LE JAUNE D'ŒUF

LA FRAISE

LE CAFÉ

LE CUILLÈRE EN BOIS

LA PLUIE

LA MARYSE

L'HEURE DU DÉJEUNER

LE SEL

LA COQUILLE
SAINT-JACQUES

RÉCHAUD À GAZ

LES CERISES

LA COUVERTURE

L'AIL

L'HERBE

LA CRÈME
CHANTILLY

UNE BOUTEILLE
DE VIN

LE FOUET

LA POÊLE

LA GOUSSE
DE VANILLE

UN VERRE
DE VIN

LES OLIVES

The little Paris kitchen

by

Rachel Khoo

The Little Paris Kitchen

120 Simple but
Classic French Recipes

Rachel Khoo

With photographs by David Loftus
and illustrations by Rachel Khoo

CHRONICLE BOOKS
SAN FRANCISCO

First published in the United States of America in 2012 by
Chronicle Books LLC.

First published in the United Kingdom in 2012 by
Michael Joseph, an imprint of Penguin Books.

Library of Congress Cataloging-in-Publication Data available.

ISBN 978-1-4521-1343-2

Manufactured in Italy

Prop styling by Elodie Rambaud

10 9 8 7 6 5 4

Chronicle Books LLC
680 Second Street
San Francisco, California 94107
www.chroniclebooks.com

Menu

Introduction

Five years ago, I made the decision to pursue my sweet dream of studying *pâtisserie* at Le Cordon Bleu. So I packed my belongings and waved goodbye to London. A short train journey across the Channel and it was *"Bonjour, Paris."*

And so my edible Parisian adventure began. The bakeries would entice me with their perfume of freshly baked baguettes and croissants. The cheese-monger would lure me with his perfectly ripe, oozing Brie displayed in the window, conveniently located next to a little wine shop. Its owner, who I nicknamed "the wine fascist," would interrogate me with a thousand questions in order to find the perfect wine match for my dinners.

The outdoor produce markets overflowed with the season's bounty, brightly colored fruits and vegetables, and the market traders would shout *"Mademoiselle, goûtez le melon. C'est délicieux!"* ("Miss, taste the melon. It's delicious!") It was a world away from the markets in London and the traders' cockney cries of "Pound of bananas, a pound!" I soaked up the French ambience in the little cafés and bistros, with the locals sipping their glasses of wine, and watched the world go by.

But discovering *la vie parisienne* wasn't just about eating it up. I had some hard work to do. During my first summer in Paris, I donned my chef's whites and enrolled at Le Cordon Bleu, the famous cookery school, for a *pâtisserie* course. I said goodbye to my style for the summer, chef's whites not being the most flattering of women's attire. Not even Kate Moss could make them look good! It was *"Oui, chef,"* for the next three months, while I learned how to make French classics like croissants and *crème brûlée*. Two hundred eggs and 40 pounds of butter, sugar, and flour later, I graduated from Le Cordon Bleu. Not quite ready to give up my sweet dream of living in Paris, I started to work at a small culinary bookstore, La Cocotte, where I baked delicious delicacies for the *salon du thé* and catered for their book launches. My little baking job led me to my current vocation as a food creative, where I develop culinary ideas for events, cookbooks, workshops, and anything else food-related. All the testing is done from the tiny little kitchen in my apartment with just a mini oven and two gas rings.

Somehow the rest of the world has forgotten how *délicieux* French food can be. The food headlines have been dominated by the molecular movement in Spain, Heston Blumenthal's edible English eccentricities, or, more recently, Scandinavia's flourishing foraging scene showcased at Noma. French cuisine has been forgone, stereotyped with the stuffy image of an old-fashioned chef laboring over a terribly complicated dish, finished with a ton of butter.

"Mais non!" I say. French flavors and techniques needn't be out of reach of the everyday home cook. Living in Paris, I eat and cook everything from simple weekday suppers to big gourmet dinners. And just because they use fancy words like *jus* or *blanchir* doesn't mean you have to have a Michelin-starred kitchen to cook great French food. I certainly don't and I've managed to cook up everything from feasts for six to girlie tea parties for eight to romantic three-course dinners for two.

My book includes all the well-known French dishes such as *boeuf bourguignon* and *coq au vin*, but it's not simply another collection of classics. It's the story of how I discovered these recipes, whether it was picnicking along the Seine on a sticky summer's night, dining with friends, or experimenting at home. I have added my own creative twist on some occasions, making this book a fresh and simple approach to French classics, perfect to share with friends and family.

Bienvenue dans ma petite cuisine à Paris!

LES ASPERGES

LA VAISSELLE

LES PIMENTS

LA CREVETTE

LES BADIANES

LE CHOU

LA COQUILLE SAINT-JACQUES

LE THYM

LES POMMES DE TERRE

LE POULET

LES POIVRONS

LE FENOUIL

LA LAVANDE

LA CARAFE D'EAU

LE FENOUIL

LES BOUGIES

LA CREVETTE

LES FEUILLES DE LAURIER

Everyday Cooking

Ma cuisine de tous les jours

LA CARAFE D'EAU

L'OIGNON

LES BADIANES

LE THYM

LA VAISSELLE

LES CAROTTES

LES BOUGIES

LA COQUILLE SAINT-JACQUES

LE CHOU

LES PIMENTS

LES POMMES DE TERRE

LES ASPERGES

There is much to be said about the daily eating habits of the French. Simplicity and *savoir-faire* and an understanding of ingredients are key. Generally, a steaming cup of *café au lait* with a sweet and comforting croissant are grabbed en route to work for breakfast. Dinners for family and friends are important events, so dishes for these occasions have a chapter of their own (see page 152), which leaves us with lunch. I wanted to call this chapter Everyday Cooking as it features simple things that are mostly eaten for lunch or supper.

L'heure de déjeuner—the French lunch hour—according to the stereotype consists of several courses, a couple of bottles of wine, and takes half an afternoon. Unfortunately the days of leisurely lunches during the week are a thing of the past as even the French aren't immune to the working culture. *Le sandwich* is, therefore, fast becoming the norm for a weekday lunch, although the French do know how to make an excellent *jambon-beurre*, also called a *parisienne*, a crusty baguette slathered in rich creamy butter with a slice of juicy ham. Not much to it, but it does beat a soggy sandwich any day.

When life does allow a longer lunch break, a visit to the local bistro or neighborhood café is the norm. The local eateries know what their customers want to eat: food to comfort the nerves after a stressful morning at the office. *Moules marinières, steak tartare, gratin dauphinois, saucisse et purée de pomme de terre avec une sauce diable* (sausages and mashed potatoes with devil's sauce), *oeufs en cocotte* (baked eggs). No fancy fussed-about food here.

While I was writing this book, I decided to test some of the recipes out on the public by opening up my own "underground" restaurant for just two diners, as my apartment is so small. People from all over the world (including the French) booked and came for lunch. It soon became clear that no matter what nationality they were, the thing they loved most was the fact that it was simple home-cooked food, not Michelin-starred gastronomy. Food that any Pierre, Paul, or Jacques (Tom, Dick, or Harry!) can cook at home.

So roll up your sleeves and get stuck into a little kitchen work or, as they say in French, *mettre la main à la pâte* (put your hand in the dough) and you'll be rewarded with an everyday meal worth sitting down to.

Salade de figues et foies de volailles

Fig and chicken liver salad

When figs appear at my local market (the best figs are available from July to September in France), I just have to buy them. Sweet, sticky, and juicy, they often don't even make it back to my kitchen—I usually gobble them all up on my way home—but if there are a few remaining, they make a delicious addition to a salad.

The sweetness of figs goes particularly well with cheese and also chicken livers. I was never a big liver fan as a kid, but they have grown on me since living in France, especially as they take literally no time to cook. Fast food *à la française*!

• 1 tbsp butter • 1 red onion, thinly sliced • 1 sprig of thyme
• 7 oz chicken livers, cleaned (if the livers are quite large, cut them in half)
• salt and pepper • 2 tbsp red wine vinegar • 4 handfuls of mixed salad leaves
• 4 figs, quartered • extra virgin olive oil, for drizzling

Melt the butter in a large nonstick frying pan and add the onion and thyme. Fry on a medium heat for 6–8 minutes or until the onion becomes soft and slightly caramelized.

Season the livers with salt and pepper. Turn the heat up to high before adding the livers to the pan, then fry for 1–2 minutes on each side or until golden brown on the outside but still pink in the middle. Add the wine vinegar at the end and let it evaporate for 30 seconds.

While the livers are cooking, scatter the salad leaves and figs on a plate.

Top the salad with the onion and livers (discarding the thyme), followed by a drizzle of olive oil and a sprinkle of salt.

Preparation time: 10 minutes Cooking time: 15 minutes

Lentilles du Puy avec un fromage de chèvre, betteraves et une vinaigrette d'aneth

Puy lentil salad with goat's cheese, beets, and a dill vinaigrette

Lentilles du Puy are grown in the sunny, volcanic Auvergne. The hot climate and mineral-rich soil give them a unique taste and texture, and they are known in France as poor man's caviar. They contain less starch than ordinary green lentils, so they hold their shape better: no mushy *lentilles du Puy*. Traditionally they are boiled in water, then fried with some chopped onion and lardons. I tend to improvise with ingredients I have in the fridge: they make a fine accompaniment to almost anything.

For the dill vinaigrette: ½ bunch of dill • 2 tbsp sunflower oil
• 2 tbsp white wine vinegar • salt • a pinch of sugar

• 1 cup Puy lentils • 1 bay leaf • 1 sprig of thyme • salt and pepper • 1 cooked beet, peeled
• a handful of baby salad leaves (optional) • 7 oz fresh soft goat's cheese* • extra virgin olive oil

TO MAKE THE VINAIGRETTE: Whizz the dill (stalks included) in a blender with the oil, vinegar, ½ tsp salt, and the sugar. Taste and add more salt if desired.

Wash the lentils in cold running water, then put them into a large pot with the bay leaf, thyme, and a generous pinch of salt. Cover the lentils with at least double their volume of boiling water and cook for 15 minutes or until tender.

Use a mandoline or a sharp knife to thinly slice the beet.

Drain the lentils and discard the bay leaf and thyme.

Divide the lentils equally between individual plates (or you could use a large serving dish) and scatter over the salad leaves (if using). Place the beet slices on top and crumble over the goat's cheese. Drizzle with the vinaigrette and a little olive oil, and finish with a sprinkling of salt and pepper.

* *If you prefer a stronger-tasting cheese, try feta or a hard goat's cheese.*

Preparation time: 20 minutes Cooking time: 15–20 minutes

Salade tiède de pommes de terre et pommes avec des miettes de boudin noir

Warm potato and apple salad with blood-sausage crumbs

Before I moved to France, the thought of eating *boudin noir* (blood sausage or black pudding) would have made my stomach turn, but now I must admit I'm quite partial to a slice or two.

If you're a *boudin noir* virgin and feel a little intimidated about eating a whole sausage, then this dish is a great way to try it because there's only a small amount and it's used like a garnish.

In France, *boudin noir* is usually partnered with cooked apples and potatoes, making it the perfect cold-weather comfort food. This recipe has the addition of mint, to give it a fresh flavor.

• 1 tsp olive oil • 8 oz firm-fleshed potatoes (such as fingerling), chopped into small cubes • salt and pepper • 1 Granny Smith apple • 1 tbsp water • 1 tsp sugar • a handful of mint leaves • 4 oz *boudin noir* or blood sausage

Put the olive oil into a pan and place on a medium heat. When the pan is warm, add the cubed potatoes and cook for 10 minutes or until the potatoes are tender and a lovely golden brown color. Shake the pan every now and again, and season the potatoes with salt and pepper.

Meanwhile, peel three-quarters of the apple and chop into small cubes (save the remainder for later). Microwave the apple cubes with the water and sugar in a covered bowl until soft. This should only take a minute or two. (Alternatively, cook for about 5 minutes in a covered small pot.)

Using the back of a spoon, mash the cooked apple to a purée, then keep the purée covered so that it stays warm.

Finely chop the mint and chop the remaining apple into small cubes (leave the skin on).

Once the potatoes are cooked, pop them into a bowl and keep them covered. Place the pan back on a medium heat. Remove the skin from the sausage and crumble the sausage meat into the pan. Cook for 2–3 minutes, tossing the crumbs so that they brown evenly.

To plate up, start by spreading a tbsp of the apple purée on each plate. Sprinkle over a little of the mint, followed by the potatoes, sausage crumbs, and chopped apple. Finally, sprinkle with a little more mint. Serve immediately.

Preparation time: 30 minutes   Cooking time: 20 minutes

Salade d'hiver avec une mousse au fromage de chèvre

Winter salad with a goat's cheese mousse

The Paris des Chefs conference is a draw for international culinary talent and is always inspirational. At the 2011 conference, I met Estonian chef Peeter Pihel (from Neh in Tallinn and Pädaste Manor on Muhu Island) and tasted one of his dishes—roasted root vegetables with a goat's cheese mousse. It inspired me to try something similar with produce from my local Parisian market.

This recipe can be adapted to any vegetables that are in season, and in summer you can use peppers, cucumbers, and tomatoes to make a crunchy raw version.

For the mousse: 7 oz *Selles-sur-Cher* cheese* • ½ cup milk • ½ cup whipping cream

For the vinaigrette: 4 tbsp sunflower or vegetable oil • 2 tbsp cider vinegar • salt

• 4 carrots, roughly chopped • 2 small dessert apples, cored and quartered
• 2 parsnips, roughly chopped • 2 tbsp sunflower oil • salt
• 3½ oz lardons or cubes of smoked bacon (optional)
• 1 cooked beet, peeled and very thinly sliced • 2 handfuls of salad leaves

TO MAKE THE MOUSSE: Beat the cheese with the milk until soft and lump free. Whip the cream to stiff peaks. Add one-quarter of the whipped cream to the cheese and mix together, then fold in the rest of the cream. Transfer the mousse to a piping bag fitted with a ⅜-inch plain nozzle and leave in the fridge until needed (it will keep for a couple of days).

TO MAKE THE VINAIGRETTE: Mix together the oil and vinegar and season with salt.

Preheat the oven to 400°F. Toss the carrots, apples, and parsnips into a large roasting pan. Drizzle with the sunflower oil and season with salt. Roast for 45 minutes or until the vegetables are tender and golden.

Just as the vegetables finish cooking, toss the lardons (if using) into a hot pan and cook until crisp.

To serve, pipe little blobs of mousse randomly all over a serving plate. Arrange the roasted vegetables and apples, beet, and salad leaves on the plate, and sprinkle the lardons (if used) on top. Finally, drizzle with the vinaigrette.

* *Selles-sur-Cher cheese works particularly well. It is a goat's cheese coated in edible ash that lends a subtle smokiness. But any other soft goat's cheese will also work.*

Preparation time: 30 minutes   Cooking time: 45 minutes

Poireaux vinaigrette avec oeuf poché et jambon de Bayonne

Leeks in vinaigrette with a poached egg and Bayonne ham

The Italians have Parma ham and the Spanish have Serrano, while the French have jambon de Bayonne, named after the city in southwest France. It is air-dried for months, while it goes through various salt-, fat-, and spice-rubbing processes to make a delicate meat that is slightly sweet and moist. Bayonne ham makes a great addition to the classic *poireaux vinaigrette*, which you don't see much any more, unless you happen to have a French *grand-mère*. Normally the leeks are boiled or steamed, but I like to pop them on the griddle pan. It brings out their sweetness.

For the vinaigrette: **6 tbsp sunflower oil** • **3 tbsp white wine vinegar** • **2 tsp grainy mustard** • **a pinch of sugar** • **salt**

• **8 young leeks** • **3 tbsp olive oil** • **1 egg per person** • **a couple of drops of vinegar** • **4 slices of Bayonne ham*** • **salt**

TO MAKE THE VINAIGRETTE: Mix together the oil, vinegar, mustard, and sugar. Season with salt.

Trim the roots from the leeks and remove the tough tops and outer leaves. Cut the leeks in half lengthwise and soak in cold water for 10 minutes, then rinse to remove any grit that may be in between the leaves.

Heat a griddle pan until smoking hot.

Brush the cut side of each leek half with olive oil, then place the leeks, cut-side down, in the pan and cook for 5 minutes or until the grill marks appear. Brush the top side of the leeks with olive oil before turning them over to cook for a further 5 minutes.

Meanwhile, bring a large pot of water to a boil. Crack an egg into a ramekin or cup and add a drop of vinegar. Whisk the boiling water vigorously before slipping in the egg, then quickly repeat with more eggs and poach for 3–4 minutes or until the yolks are just set and slightly soft.

To assemble, divide the leeks between individual plates and drizzle the vinaigrette on top.** Shred the ham into strips and drape over the leeks. Top each serving with a poached egg and a sprinkling of salt.

 * *Can be substituted with Serrano or Parma ham.*

** *The leeks and vinaigrette can be served on their own as a hot side dish, or cold the next day.*

Preparation time: 30 minutes Cooking time: 20 minutes

Oeufs en meurette

Poached eggs in a red wine sauce

This is a pretty classy way to serve a humble poached egg for an indulgent brunch or starter for lunch. Both the sauce and the eggs can be prepared a day in advance.

*For the red wine sauce:** 1 onion, finely chopped • 1 stick of celery, finely chopped • 1 carrot, finely chopped • 1 oz lardons or cubes of smoked bacon • 2 tbsp butter • ¼ cup all-purpose flour • 2 cups veal or beef stock, warm • 1 tbsp tomato paste • ¾ cup red wine • 1 bouquet garni (thyme, bay leaf, parsley stalks, peppercorns)

• 4 fresh eggs** • a couple of drops of vinegar • toast for serving

TO MAKE THE SAUCE: Fry the vegetables and lardons on a medium heat until golden. Remove them from the pan with a slotted spoon, then add the butter. Melt over a medium heat, sprinkle in the flour, and stir constantly until it turns an almost Coca-Cola color. Turn the heat down to low and slowly pour in the warm stock, whisking energetically. Add the tomato paste and wine and whisk until the paste has dissolved. Pop the fried vegetables and lardons back into the pan, add the bouquet garni, and simmer gently for 15 minutes. Pour the sauce through a sieve and taste for seasoning, then pour into a clean pan and gently heat through.

Meanwhile, pour water into a deep, wide frying pan until about 3¼ inches deep and bring to a boil. Crack each egg into a ramekin or cup and add a drop of vinegar. Whisk the boiling water vigorously before quickly slipping in the eggs one after the other. Turn the heat down and simmer for 3–4 minutes or until the yolks are just set and slightly soft.

Remove the eggs from the water with a slotted spoon and serve on hot toast, with the sauce poured over and around.***

* For a fiery sauce, add 10 cracked black peppercorns.

** The key to successful poaching is to use the freshest eggs possible. Old eggs will have ragged, feathery whites, whereas the white on a fresh egg will hold together.

*** To make in advance, put the poached eggs into a bowl of ice-cold water and pour the sauce into an airtight container. Keep both in the fridge. Reheat the sauce before serving, and warm the eggs through by lowering them into boiling water with a slotted spoon. Simmer for 30 seconds.

Preparation time: 15 minutes Cooking time: 30 minutes

Oeufs en cocotte

Eggs in pots

Two main ingredients—eggs and crème fraîche—are all you need for this super-simple yet very tasty dish. You can glam it up with a drizzle of truffle oil at the end if you like, or with a few thin shavings of real truffle.

I usually take a look in my fridge and throw in whatever I find suitable (which is almost anything savory). Serve with plenty of crusty bread or, for a gluten-free alternative, try steamed asparagus, raw carrot, bell pepper, or cucumber sticks.

Traditionally ramekins are used for baking *oeufs en cocotte*, but I make mine in teacups to add a little British touch to this classic French dish.

• ⅔ cup crème fraîche* • salt and pepper • nutmeg • a handful of chopped dill**
• 4 eggs • red lumpfish roe • small sprigs of dill

Preheat the oven to 350°F. Season the crème fraîche with salt, pepper, and a pinch of nutmeg. Place a heaped tablespoon of crème fraîche in the bottom of a ramekin, followed by a little dill. Crack an egg on top, add a second tbsp of crème fraîche, and sprinkle with a pinch each of salt, pepper, and nutmeg. Repeat with three more ramekins.

Place the ramekins in a baking dish and pour enough lukewarm water into the dish to come halfway up the sides of the ramekins. Bake for 15 minutes or until the egg yolks are set to your liking.

If you like, finish each serving with a teaspoon of red lumpfish roe and a sprig or two of dill.

Some alternative ideas:

  * *The crème fraîche can be replaced with* Sauce Béchamel *or* Sauce Mornay *(page 269). If you like, you can add chopped mushrooms, ham, smoked salmon, or cherry tomatoes after the crème fraîche, or a spoonful of* piperade *(see page 30).*

** *Try swapping the dill for parsley, basil, or cilantro, or spice things up with a dash of Tabasco or chile sauce.*

Preparation time: 10 minutes Baking time: 15 minutes

Omelette soufflée et piperade

Soufflé omelette with a Basque pepper relish

The Basque region in the western Pyrenees has a strong identity, which is reflected in its food. In *piperade*, the colors of tomatoes, green bell pepper, and onion represent the red, green, and white of the Basque flag.

Traditionally, *piperade* is made with eggs that are simply scrambled into the dish, but I like to go the extra mile and serve it as a fluffy soufflé omelette.

For the piperade: 2 tbsp olive oil • 1 clove of garlic, crushed to a paste
• 1 onion, thinly sliced • 1 sprig of thyme • 1 green bell pepper, seeded and thinly sliced
• ½ tsp ground Espelette pepper* or a pinch of regular chile powder
• 2 tomatoes, roughly chopped • a pinch of sugar • salt

For the soufflé omelette: 4 eggs, separated • a pinch of salt • 1 tbsp butter

TO MAKE THE *PIPERADE*:** Place a large nonstick pan on a medium heat and put the olive oil, garlic, onion, and thyme into the pan. When the onion begins to soften, throw in the bell pepper, Espelette pepper, and tomatoes. Cover and cook for 10 minutes or until the bell pepper is soft.

Meanwhile, preheat the oven to 350°F and make the soufflé omelette. Put the egg whites and salt into a bowl and beat until stiff. In a separate large bowl, beat the egg yolks for a minute. Fold half the egg whites into the egg yolks until evenly incorporated, then fold in the rest.

Place a large nonstick frying pan (that can go in the oven) on a medium heat. Melt the butter until it begins to sizzle, then pour in the eggs and spread them quickly with a palette knife to cover the bottom of the pan. Cook for 3–4 minutes, then place in the oven and bake for 4 minutes.

To serve, loosen the omelette from the bottom of the pan with the palette knife. Invert a large plate on top of the pan, then turn the pan and plate over so the omelette comes out on the plate. Remove the sprig of thyme from the piperade, add the sugar, and taste for salt. Spread the *piperade* on top of the omelette and serve immediately.

* *Espelette pepper is cultivated in the Basque country, which is why it's so commonly used in the cuisine of this region. Don't be misled by its bright orange-red color—it is slightly less fiery then chile (but it does have a bit more kick than regular pepper).*

** *The* piperade *can be made up to 3 days in advance and kept in the fridge, then reheated before spreading on top of the omelette. It is also good served cold with crusty bread or a dollop of crème fraîche.*

Preparation time: 10 minutes Cooking time: 20 minutes

Soupe au pistou

Pistou soup

Soup is not just for cold winter nights, it's great for hot summer days, too. *Soupe au pistou*, from Provence, is jam-packed with summer vegetables and is served with a sauce—the *pistou* part. *Pistou* is a distant relative of the Italian pesto, except that *pistou* traditionally has no pine nuts or Parmesan cheese (the word originates from the Provençal dialect and means *pounded*). If you don't have a mortar and pestle for the pounding, some simple whizzing in a blender will give you a pretty good result, too. Maybe the modern version should be called *soupe au whizzou?*

For a classic pistou: 1 bunch of basil • 3 cloves of garlic • 3–4 tbsp good extra virgin olive oil

For a Vietnamese pistou: 1 bunch of Vietnamese basil • 1 stalk of lemongrass, roughly chopped
• ½ small red chile, seeded • 5 tbsp sunflower oil

• 3 tbsp olive oil • 2 onions, diced • 4 cloves of garlic, crushed to a paste • 1 sprig of thyme
• 2 bay leaves • 4 tbsp tomato paste • 2 carrots, diced • 2 zucchini, diced
• 7 oz green beans, quartered • 14-oz can white beans (e.g., haricots blancs, cannellini),
drained and rinsed • 2 qt boiling water • 1 tbsp salt • a pinch of sugar
• pepper • ⅔ cup dried pasta (a small variety like orzo) • 1¼ cups fresh or frozen peas

To make a *pistou*, simply pound the ingredients to a smooth paste (or whizz in a blender).

Heat the olive oil in a large pot. Add the onions and garlic and cook gently, stirring occasionally, until soft and translucent. Add the thyme, bay leaves, tomato paste, carrots, and zucchini, then cook for 15–20 minutes or until the vegetables are al dente (tender but still a little crunchy). Add the green and white beans with the boiling water and bring to a boil, then add the pasta and peas. Cook for 10 minutes or until the pasta is al dente. Remove the sprig of thyme and the bay leaves, then add the salt and sugar and season with pepper. Serve immediately, with a dollop of the *pistou*.

Pourquoi a Vietnamese *pistou?*

This spicy *pistou* is a homage to Le Grain de Riz, one of my favorite Vietnamese restaurants in Paris (if you can call it a restaurant—it only seats 12 people). When Vietnam was a French colony, the Vietnamese adopted the baguette, and a popular snack is *bánh mì*, a baguette filled with mayonnaise, various pickled vegetables, and grilled meat. Now it seems the tables have turned, and the Vietnamese community in France is influencing the French culinary scene with cheap and cheerful *cantines* popping up everywhere.

Preparation time: 30 minutes   Cooking time: 35–40 minutes

Gratin dauphinois

Creamy potato bake

To rinse or not to rinse the potatoes, that is the question that pops up in many *gratin dauphinois* recipes. It all depends whether you're using firm or baking potatoes. Baking ones will release their starch into the cream and make the gratin bind, whereas I prefer firm potatoes as they hold their shape better (no gratin mush for me). I like my gratin to be dense with crunchy, crisp edges, but you could always conduct some potato experiments of your own. All for research purposes, of course, not the fact that it's so delicious . . .

• 2 lb firm-fleshed potatoes (such as fingerling) • 1¼ cups milk • 1¼ cups heavy cream
• a pinch of nutmeg • 1 tsp Dijon mustard • 1 tsp salt • 1 clove of garlic
• 2 tbsp soft butter • chopped parsley or dill (optional)

Peel the potatoes and cut them into ⅛-inch-thick slices. Place them in a pot with the milk, cream, nutmeg, mustard, and salt and simmer for 10 minutes.

Meanwhile, preheat the oven to 400°F. Cut the clove of garlic in half and rub the cut sides around the inside of a baking dish, then smear the butter around the inside of the dish.

Pour the potato and cream mix into the dish and spread the potatoes out evenly. Bake for 35–40 minutes or until golden and bubbling. Serve hot, topped with a sprinkling of chopped parsley, and a simple green salad.

For a light lunch or dinner for 4–6 people

Stir 7 ounces chopped smoked salmon, the finely grated zest of a lemon, and a handful of chopped dill into the potato mix before baking.

Preparation time: 15 minutes Cooking time: 45–50 minutes

Nids de tartiflette

Cheese and potato nests

The *tartiflette* recipe was the brainchild of the Reblochon cheese producers in the 1980s. With so many other French cheeses to compete with, they needed to find a way of making theirs more popular, and they did it with this cheesy potato gratin.

Reblochon is a cheese that comes from the Haute-Savoie in the Alps. It's made out of raw cow's milk and has a pungent aroma and nutty taste. If you can't find Reblochon, or you prefer a milder flavor, replace it with Brie and make a *Brieflette* (doesn't have quite the same ring, though, does it?).

Traditionally this dish is quite a heavy winter staple, but make it my way and you can even serve it on a hot day with a side salad.

• 1 tbsp soft butter • 1 lb firm-fleshed potatoes (such as fingerling)
• 1 onion, finely chopped • 1 clove of garlic, finely chopped • 1 bay leaf
• 7 oz lardons or cubes of smoked bacon • 6½ tbsp dry white wine
• 8-oz piece of Reblochon cheese, cubed

Preheat the oven to 375°F and brush a 6-cup muffin tin with the butter. Peel the potatoes and use the julienne blade on a mandoline to make thin matchsticks (or slice by hand).

Put the onion, garlic, bay leaf, and lardons into a large nonstick frying pan and cook until the lardons are golden. Add the wine and reduce until only a couple of tablespoons of liquid remain. Stir in the potato matchsticks and take off the heat, then remove the bay leaf and stir in the Reblochon cubes.

Divide the potato mix between the cups in the muffin tin and bake for 15–20 minutes or until golden and bubbling. Serve immediately.

Preparation time: 30 minutes Baking time: 15–20 minutes

Gratin de choufleur avec une chapelure aux noisettes

Cauliflower bake with hazelnut crunch crust

Béchamel sauce with the addition of cheese (called *sauce Mornay* by the French) can only be a good thing. Coat any kind of vegetable with this sauce, and it'll get vegetable-hating kids licking their plates clean. A sneaky little trick I learned during my years working as a nanny.

The cauliflower can easily be replaced with broccoli, sliced zucchini, squash, or even potatoes.

For the Mornay (cheese) sauce: 2 tbsp butter • ¼ cup all-purpose flour • 2 cups milk, lukewarm • ¼ onion, skin removed • 1 clove • 1 bay leaf • a pinch each of white pepper and nutmeg • salt • 7 oz Gruyère, mature Comté, or Parmesan cheese, grated

• 3-lb head of cauliflower, trimmed and separated into florets (about 2 lb when trimmed) • ⅓ cup hazelnuts, finely chopped • 1 slice of extra-crunchy toast, roughly chopped

TO MAKE THE SAUCE: Melt the butter in a large pan over a medium heat. Add the flour and beat hard until you have a smooth paste. Take off the heat and leave to cool for 2 minutes, then gradually add the milk, whisking constantly. Place the pan back over a medium heat, add the onion, clove, and bay leaf, and simmer gently for 10 minutes, whisking frequently. If the sauce becomes too thick, whisk in a little more milk. Finish the sauce by removing the onion, clove, and bay leaf, then add the pepper and nutmeg and salt to taste. Leave to cool slightly.

Steam the cauliflower using either a steamer basket or a colander fitted inside a pan. Cooking time depends on how you like your cauliflower cooked—I like mine on the crunchy side, which takes about 15 minutes.

Preheat the oven to 350°F.

Stir the cheese into the warm sauce (save a little to sprinkle on top of the gratin), then mix the sauce with the cauliflower and spoon into individual baking dishes.* Sprinkle with the rest of the cheese followed by the hazelnuts and toast crumbs. Bake for 10 minutes, then pop under a hot broiler for a few minutes to get a golden, bubbling crust. Serve immediately.

* *Or bake in one large dish for 20 minutes, followed by about 5 minutes under the broiler.*

Preparation time: 30 minutes   Cooking time: 30 minutes

Gratin de macaronis au fromage

Mac 'n' cheese

My first job in Paris was taking care of two girls, Kami and Loïs. Cooking for French taste buds is daunting enough, and cooking for kids can be even harder, but this dish was a winner every time I made it. A great thing considering how easy it is to make, with ingredients that you're most likely to have on hand in the kitchen.

For the béchamel *sauce:* **2 tbsp butter • ¼ cup all-purpose flour • 2 cups milk, lukewarm • ¼ onion, skin removed • 1 clove • 1 bay leaf • a pinch of nutmeg • salt and white pepper**

• **10 oz (2½–3 cups) macaroni • 7 oz Gruyère, mature Comté, or Parmesan cheese,* grated**

TO MAKE THE *BÉCHAMEL* SAUCE: Melt the butter in a large pan over a medium heat. Add the flour and beat hard until you have a smooth paste. Take off the heat and leave to cool for 2 minutes, then gradually add the milk, whisking constantly. Place the pan back over a medium heat, add the onion, clove, and bay leaf, and simmer gently for 10 minutes, whisking frequently. If the sauce becomes too thick, whisk in a little more milk.

Finish the sauce by removing the onion, clove, and bay leaf, then adding the nutmeg and seasoning with salt and white pepper (although black pepper is fine if you don't mind the speckles). Leave to cool slightly.

Preheat the oven to 350°F. Cook the pasta according to package instructions.

Drain the pasta and tip into a large baking dish.

Save a handful of cheese to sprinkle on the top at the end, then mix the rest into the warm sauce.** Pour the sauce over the pasta and mix until the pasta is well coated. Sprinkle the rest of the cheese on top and bake for 20 minutes until bubbly and golden. Serve immediately.

 * *Pourquoi?* *It's important to use a strong-flavored cheese, as you will need less cheese to give the sauce a good flavor.*

** *Make sure you add the cheese when the sauce is warm rather than hot. If the sauce is too hot, the fat will separate from the protein and form a layer on top.*

Preparation time: 15 minutes Cooking time: 35 minutes

Ratatouille

Provençal vegetable stew

How to make a *ratatouille* can be a touchy subject at dinner parties in France, with everyone claiming their recipe is the best. Some people prefer to cook each vegetable individually and mix everything together at the end, others prefer to throw it all in a pot, and then there are some who like to carefully arrange the vegetables and make a sort of gratin. At the end of the day it all depends whether you like your *ratatouille* soft and jammy or with a bit of bite.

Of course, being someone who wants to have it all, I like my *ratatouille* to tick both boxes. Partially cooking the vegetables on top of the stove and then baking everything together in the oven gives you the best of both worlds—creamy soft onion and tomatoes, with freshness and crunch from the zucchini and peppers.

• 1 clove of garlic, crushed to a paste • 1 onion, finely chopped • 1 sprig of thyme, leaves only
• 3 tbsp olive oil, plus extra for drizzling • 1 eggplant, thinly sliced* • 1 zucchini, thinly sliced*
• 1 red bell pepper, seeded and thinly sliced • 1 yellow bell pepper, seeded and thinly sliced
• 6 tomatoes, cut into quarters • a pinch of sugar • salt

Preheat the oven to 350°F. Gently fry the garlic, onion, and thyme leaves in 2 tablespoons of the olive oil. Once the onion is translucent and soft, add the eggplant and continue to cook until soft (roughly 5 minutes).

Toss the remaining vegetables in a large roasting pan with another tablespoon of olive oil. Add the cooked onion and eggplant and mix together.

Cover the roasting pan with aluminum foil (making sure the foil doesn't touch the vegetables) or with parchment paper. Bake for an hour, then stir the vegetables a little and add the sugar. Taste for salt. Set under a hot broiler for 3–4 minutes or until the top layer of vegetables is caramelized around the edges. Drizzle with olive oil and serve warm, or cold the next day.

* A mandoline makes an easy job of cutting vegetables into thin slices.

Preparation time: 30 minutes Cooking time: 1¼ hours

Lapin croustillant à la moutarde de Meaux

Crispy rabbit with Meaux mustard

It was the Romans who introduced mustard seeds to the Gauls; and by the ninth century, monasteries all over France were making money from selling mustard. The stone quarries in the Meaux region provided the millstones to grind the mustard seeds, turning the area into one of the top French mustard producers, and yet *moutarde de Meaux* is probably less well known than its southern relative—the spicy yellow mustard from Dijon.

Unlike Dijon mustard, which is creamy, the grains in the traditional mustard from Meaux are only partially ground, giving it a crunch that makes a great crispy crust when combined with breadcrumbs.

- 2 tbsp vegetable or sunflower oil • 4 rabbit legs*
- 4 heaped tbsp Meaux mustard or another grainy mustard
- ½ to 1 cup breadcrumbs (fresh or dried)

Preheat the oven to 400°F. Swirl the oil around a baking sheet and place in the oven to get hot.

Meanwhile, brush the rabbit legs with plenty of mustard and then press the breadcrumbs onto the mustard to coat the rabbit evenly.

Place the rabbit legs on the hot baking sheet and roast for 30 minutes or until cooked through. The juices should run clear, not red or pink, when a thick part of the flesh is pierced with the tip of a sharp knife. Serve hot.

* *Chicken legs are also good cooked this way.*

Preparation time: 15 minutes Cooking time: 30 minutes

Moules marinières

Mussels with white wine

There's not much you need to make *moules marinières*. Add a splash of white wine to some softened onion, throw in the mussels, and finish with a dollop of crème fraîche and some crusty bread—that's more or less it. Who said French food was complicated?

• 4 lb mussels • 1 onion, thinly sliced • 1 bulb of fennel, thinly sliced* • 1 tbsp butter
• 1 bay leaf • 2 sprigs of thyme or a pinch of dried thyme • ⅔ cup dry white wine
• ⅔ cup crème fraîche • a handful of chopped parsley

Clean the mussels using plenty of cold water. Pull out the fibrous beards and scrub off any barnacles. Toss any that have cracked or broken shells, or that do not close when lightly squeezed.

In a large pot (big enough to hold all the mussels with some extra room to spare), soften the onion and fennel over a low heat with the butter, bay leaf, and thyme. When the onion and fennel are soft and translucent, add the wine followed by the cleaned mussels. Increase the heat to high, cover the pan, and cook for 3–4 minutes or until the mussels open, shaking the pan a few times to help them cook evenly.

At the end of the cooking time, remove the bay leaf and sprigs of thyme (if used) and discard any mussels that have not opened. Stir in the crème fraîche and serve immediately, with a sprinkling of chopped parsley.

* *I've included the fennel because it adds a subtle aniseed flavor that goes extremely well with the white wine and crème fraîche, but you don't have to use it.*

Preparation time: 15 minutes Cooking time: 10 minutes

Gratin au poisson fumé

Smoky fish bake

This easy bake makes good use of leftover cooked potatoes. You can also mix in leftover vegetables such as zucchini, carrots, broccoli, and cauliflower.

For the béchamel *sauce:* 2 tbsp butter • ¼ cup all-purpose flour • 2 cups milk, lukewarm • ¼ onion, skin removed • 1 clove • 1 bay leaf • a pinch of nutmeg • salt and white pepper

• 1½ lb (8–10 medium) potatoes, peeled and already cooked (you can use leftover roast potatoes) • 7 oz smoked haddock, skin removed • a handful of chopped parsley • a handful of grated mature cheese, e.g., Gruyère, Comté, Parmesan, or mature Cheddar

TO MAKE THE *BÉCHAMEL* SAUCE: Melt the butter in a large pan over a medium heat. Add the flour and beat hard until you have a smooth paste. Take off the heat and leave to cool for 2 minutes, then gradually add the milk, whisking constantly. Place the pan back over a medium heat, add the onion, clove, and bay leaf, and simmer gently for 10 minutes, whisking frequently. If the sauce becomes too thick, whisk in a little more milk. Finish the sauce by removing the onion, clove, and bay leaf, then adding the nutmeg and seasoning with salt and white pepper (although black pepper is fine if you don't mind the speckles). Leave to cool slightly.

Preheat the oven to 350°F.

Slice the potatoes into ¼-inch-thick rounds. Cut or flake the haddock into small chunks and add to the *béchamel* sauce with most of the parsley (save a little for garnish). Mix together, then add the potatoes. Pour into a baking dish, sprinkle with a little grated cheese, and bake for 20 minutes or until golden. Garnish with a little chopped parsley before serving.

Preparation time: 15 minutes   Cooking time: 35 minutes

Truite en papillote avec fenouil, citron et crème fraîche

Trout in a parcel with lemon, fennel, and crème fraîche

Papillote sounds a lot more fancy than it actually is—ingredients simply popped into a paper parcel and then baked. The only thing to remember is to seal your parcel well, so that none of the delicious juices can escape.

• 10 oz baby potatoes, scrubbed • 4 tbsp extra virgin olive oil
• finely grated zest of 1 lemon • salt and pepper
• 2 freshwater trout, cleaned and gutted (with bones left in)
• 1 bulb of fennel, thinly sliced • 4 heaped tbsp crème fraîche • lemon wedges

Steam the potatoes until almost tender, roughly 10 minutes. Leave until cool enough to handle, then slice. Preheat the oven to 325°F.

Mix the olive oil with the lemon zest and 1 teaspoon salt and season with pepper. Rub this mixture inside the fish.

Place each trout on a large sheet of parchment paper and stuff with the fennel slices. Place the sliced potatoes on the paper, alongside the fish. Now bring the edges of the paper together and fold over to form a sealed parcel, tucking the ends underneath. You may need to use kitchen string or aluminum foil to keep each parcel closed.

Bake for 15–20 minutes, depending on the thickness of the fish. To test for doneness, open a parcel and lift up the skin of the fish—the flesh should look opaque, not translucent, and flake easily with a fork. Serve with the juices from the parcels, the crème fraîche, and lemon wedges.

Preparation time: 15 minutes Cooking time: 25–30 minutes

Tartare de maquereau avec un condiment rhubarbe et concombre

Mackerel tartare with a rhubarb and cucumber relish

Mackerel makes a wonderful alternative to the classic salmon *tartare* seen on French bistro menus. Cucumber adds a crunch factor and the acidic note of the raw rhubarb cuts through the oiliness of the fish. Don't worry about eating raw rhubarb. It's the leaves that are poisonous, not the stalks.

For the relish: 1 stick of rhubarb, finely diced
• 1 small cucumber, finely diced • 1 tbsp freshly squeezed lemon juice
• 1 tbsp cider vinegar • a pinch of salt • 1 tsp sugar, or to taste

• 4 mackerel fillets, skinned* • a pinch of salt • 1 tbsp extra virgin olive oil, for drizzling

MAKE THE RELISH: Mix all the ingredients together. Leave to stand for 10 minutes.

Meanwhile, check the fish for any bones before cutting into very small dice. Put the diced fish into a bowl, season with the salt and olive oil, and mix together. Serve immediately, with the relish and a drizzle of olive oil.

* *It's essential to use the freshest mackerel possible. I buy my mackerel whole so that I can see how fresh the fish is. Here are a few tips on how to tell whether fish is fresh:*
  • *bright, shiny eyes*
  • *glossy skin*
  • *it doesn't smell "fishy"*
  • *If you look under the gills, they should be a rich red. Faded, dull red means the fish is old.*

Preparation time: 20 minutes

Steak tartare

Steak tartare

There's honestly not much to making *steak tartare*. A good-quality fillet of beef, minced or chopped, with some condiments: *c'est tout!*

Some bistros serve their *tartares* already seasoned and with the condiments mixed into the meat. I prefer the easier option of just serving the condiments on the side. This way, everyone can customize their *tartare* to their own taste.

> • 1⅔ lb very fresh beef fillet, minced or finely chopped by hand • 4 fresh egg yolks*
> • pepper (optional) • 4 tbsp capers, finely chopped • 2 shallots, finely chopped
> • 8 cornichons, finely chopped • ½ bunch of parsley, finely chopped • Dijon mustard
> • Tabasco • Worcestershire sauce • Crusty bread

Divide the beef between four plates, using your hands to form the meat into patties. Top each tartare with an egg yolk, and sprinkle with pepper if you like. Put the chopped condiments into little bowls, and pop the mustard, Tabasco, and Worcestershire sauce on the table for everyone to help themselves. Serve with some crusty bread.

* *This classic* steak tartare *is served with a raw egg yolk, but I prefer mine without, as I find the egg too rich with the meat.*

Japanese twist

Try the following Japanese accompaniments instead of the classic condiments above.

> • 1 tbsp sugar • 5 tbsp rice wine vinegar • 1 small cucumber, cut into very small cubes
> • 2 daikon (white radishes), about 8 in long, cut into very small cubes

Dissolve the sugar in the rice wine vinegar. Stir in the cucumber and radish. Leave to marinate for 30 minutes, stirring occasionally. Serve with some pickled Japanese ginger and a small dab of wasabi paste.

Preparation time: 10–15 minutes
Resting time: 30 minutes (for the Japanese condiment)

Bouillon de poulet avec des quenelles de volailles

Chicken dumpling soup

Soup for your soul, or for when you're ill. My Austrian grandma used to make a chicken dumpling soup that I always crave when I'm feeling a little under the weather. Dumplings (or *quenelles* in French) are traditionally served with a heavy sauce, but I think they go just as well in this light soup.

For the quenelles*:* 7 oz raw chicken breast • 3½ oz white bread, no crusts • 6½ tbsp half-and-half • 1 egg plus 1 egg yolk • 1 tsp salt • a pinch of pepper • a pinch of nutmeg

• 6½ cups chicken stock • 2 large carrots, roughly chopped
• 5 button mushrooms, thinly sliced • salt and pepper (if needed)*
• ½ bunch of parsley, leaves roughly chopped

TO MAKE THE *QUENELLES*: Put all the ingredients into a blender and whizz until you have a smooth paste. Form the paste into 20–25 *quenelle* shapes by using two tablespoons (for smaller *quenelles*, use two teaspoons).

Put the stock and carrots into a large pot. Bring the stock to a boil and boil for 10 minutes.

Drop the *quenelles* into the boiling stock and cook for 5 minutes (3 minutes for the small ones), adding the mushrooms for the last minute. When the *quenelles* are done, they will rise to the surface. Serve immediately, garnished with some roughly chopped parsley.

* *Depending on the quality of your stock, you may not need to add any salt or pepper. Taste for seasoning before serving.*

The traditional way with *quenelles*

Poach the *quenelles* in boiling water until they rise to the surface, then drain and put into a baking dish. Cover with grated cheese or *Sauce Béchamel* (page 269) and broil until the top is bubbling and golden.

Preparation time: 30 minutes Cooking time: 20 minutes

Navarin d'agneau printanier

Spring lamb stew

For the fashion-conscious, the arrival of spring in Paris means that it's out with the winter ward-robe and in with the spring one. The same goes for stews. Forget your winter *boeuf bourguignon*; it's so last season! *Navarin printanier*, a lamb stew with fresh spring vegetables, is what should be bubbling away in your kitchen.

• 2 lb lamb neck, cut into 6 pieces • 2 cloves of garlic, crushed to a paste • 1 onion, finely chopped
• 1 tbsp olive oil • 1 bay leaf • 2 sprigs of thyme • 4 carrots, cut into chunks
• ¾ cup fresh or frozen peas • 3½ oz green beans, chopped • salt and pepper

Preheat the oven to 325°F. Brown the meat, garlic, and onion with the olive oil in a large Dutch oven. Add the bay leaf, thyme, and carrots, and enough water to cover the meat by at least an inch. Bring to a simmer and remove any foam that rises to the top. Once all the foam is removed, cover the pan and transfer to the oven. Cook for 1½–2 hours or until the meat is tender.

Ten minutes before serving, bring a large pot of salted water to a boil and add the peas and beans. Cook for 5 minutes or until the vegetables are tender, then drain.

Take the casserole out of the oven and remove the bay leaf and sprigs of thyme. Add the peas and beans to the lamb, season with salt and pepper, and serve straightaway.

For an English twist

Serve the stew with some mint sauce.

Preparation time: 30 minutes   Cooking time: 1½–2 hours

Hachis Parmentier tricolore

Three-colored "shepherd's pie"

I thought *hachis Parmentier* was a French take on English shepherd's pie until I realized it doesn't use ground meat but leftover meat from a stew or roast. Antoine-Augustin Parmentier was an eighteenth-century French pharmacist who championed the humble potato. Previously used as animal fodder, Parmentier put potatoes on the French culinary map by promoting them as a nutritious vegetable at high-society banquets and dinners. *Hachis Parmentier* with its mashed-potato topping is an homage to the man who made potatoes fashionable. This is my colorful version.

For the topping: 1 lb squash, peeled and cut into chunks • olive oil • salt • nutmeg
• 1 lb baking potatoes (such as russets or Yukon Gold) • ½ bunch of parsley
• ½ cup milk • 1 tbsp butter • white pepper

• 3 shallots, thinly sliced • 2 cloves of garlic, crushed to a paste • 1 carrot, finely diced
• 1 bay leaf • 1 sprig of thyme (leaves only) • 1 tbsp olive oil • 2 tbsp tomato paste
• 10 oz roast or stewed meat,* shredded • 6½ cups vegetable stock, plus a little extra if needed
• a pinch of sugar • salt and pepper

TO MAKE THE TOPPING: Preheat the oven to 400°F. Toss the squash chunks into a large roasting pan and drizzle with olive oil. Roast for 20 minutes or until tender. Whizz to a smooth paste in the blender, then season to taste with salt and nutmeg. Spoon into a piping bag or a heavy-duty food bag.

Cook the potatoes in a large pot of boiling salted water for 15–20 minutes or until tender. In a blender, whizz the parsley (including the stalks) with 3 tablespoons olive oil until smooth. Once the potatoes are cooked, drain and mash until smooth with the milk and butter. Season with nutmeg, salt, and white pepper. Split into two equal portions and mix the parsley paste into one. Spoon each portion of potatoes into a piping bag or heavy-duty food bag.

Fry the shallots, garlic, carrot, bay leaf, and thyme with the olive oil until the shallots are translucent and soft. Add the tomato paste, meat, stock, and sugar; season with salt and pepper; and cook for a further 5 minutes.

To assemble, pour the meat mixture into a large baking dish and cover with piped lines of the different toppings. (If you're using food bags for the piping, cut a corner off each bag and squeeze the potatoes out at the corner.) Bake for 30 minutes or until bubbling and golden. Serve hot.

* *You could use leftovers from a* Pot-au-feu *(see page 199).*

Preparation time: 45 minutes Cooking time: 1 hour

Boulettes de viande avec une sauce piquante et des pâtes d'Alsace

Meatballs in spicy sauce with Alsatian pasta

Pasta is not what comes to mind when you think of French food, but Alsace (the French region bordering Germany) is renowned for its egg pasta. Most pasta is made of hard wheat flour and water, whereas Alsatian pasta is made from hard wheat flour and fresh eggs.

For the spicy sauce: * 1 onion, finely chopped • 1 carrot, finely chopped
• 1 stick of celery, finely chopped • 1 oz lardons or cubes of smoked bacon • 2 tbsp butter
• ¼ cup all-purpose flour • 2 cups veal or beef stock, warm • 1 tbsp tomato paste
• ¾ cup red wine • 1 bouquet garni (thyme, bay leaf, parsley stalks, peppercorns)
• 2 tbsp cornichons, finely chopped • 2 tbsp capers, finely chopped

• 8 oz ground sausage (or sausage with casings removed) • 8 oz ground beef • 1 tbsp olive oil
• 12 oz pasta, preferably Alsatian egg pasta • chopped parsley, to garnish

TO MAKE THE SAUCE: Fry the vegetables and lardons on a medium heat until golden. Remove them from the pan with a slotted spoon, then add the butter. Melt over a medium heat, sprinkle in the flour, and stir constantly until it turns an almost Coca-Cola color. Turn the heat down to low and slowly pour in the warm stock, whisking energetically. Add the tomato paste and wine and whisk until the paste has dissolved. Pop the fried vegetables and lardons back into the pan, add the bouquet garni, and simmer gently for 15 minutes. Pour the sauce through a sieve and add the chopped cornichons and capers. Taste for seasoning and set aside until needed.**

Meanwhile, mix together the sausage meat and beef. Form balls slightly smaller than a golf ball. Fry in a large nonstick frying pan with the olive oil for about 5 minutes or until cooked through. Pour the sauce over the meatballs, stir together, and heat through.

Cook the pasta according to the package instructions. Drain and serve with the meatballs in the sauce, sprinkled with a little chopped parsley.

 * *You can make a creamy sauce instead, by simply adding 2 tablespoons each finely chopped cornichons and capers to Sauce Béchamel (page 269). It goes just as well with the meatballs as the spicy sauce.*

** *The sauce (without the capers and cornichons) will keep for several days in an airtight container in the fridge, and it can also be frozen.*

Preparation time: 30 minutes Cooking time: 30 minutes

Saucisse et purée de pomme de terre avec une sauce diable

Bangers 'n' mash with devil's gravy

My butcher makes great sausages. The perfect way to serve them? With mashed potatoes and gravy, in this case *sauce diable*, an *espagnole sauce* with white wine, shallots, and cayenne pepper.

For the sauce diable: 1 onion, finely chopped • 1 carrot, finely chopped
• 1 stick of celery, finely chopped • 1 oz lardons or cubes of smoked bacon • 2 tbsp butter
• ¼ cup all-purpose flour • 2 cups veal or beef stock, warm • 1 tbsp tomato paste
• ¾ cup dry white wine • 1 bouquet garni (thyme, bay leaf, parsley stalks, peppercorns)
• a pinch of cayenne pepper

For the mash: 1½ lb baking potatoes (e.g., russet or Yukon Gold), peeled
• 4 tbsp butter • ½ to ¾ cup milk, lukewarm • nutmeg • salt

• 2 tbsp butter • 4 shallots, finely sliced • 8 sausages

TO MAKE THE SAUCE: Fry the vegetables and lardons on a medium heat until golden. Remove them from the pan (try and keep as much of the fat as possible in the pan), then add the butter. Melt over a medium heat, sprinkle in the flour, and stir constantly until it turns an almost Coca-Cola color. Turn the heat down to low and slowly pour in the warm stock, whisking energetically. Add the tomato paste and wine and whisk until the paste has dissolved. Pop the fried vegetables and lardons back into the pan, add the bouquet garni, and simmer gently for 15 minutes. Pour the sauce through a sieve, add the cayenne, and taste for seasoning. Set aside until needed.*

TO MAKE THE MASH: Put the potatoes on to boil in salted water for 15–20 minutes until tender.

Drain the potatoes, put back into the pan, and heat, stirring constantly, until dry. Once the potatoes have stopped steaming, push them through a potato ricer or food mill. Mix with the butter and add enough warm milk to make a smooth, creamy mash. Season with nutmeg and a little salt.

Meanwhile, melt the butter in a large nonstick frying pan and fry the shallots until soft. Add the shallots to the sauce and use the same pan to fry the sausages for 6–8 minutes or until cooked through. Turn them occasionally so that they become evenly browned on all sides.

To serve, reheat the sauce and pour over the sausages and mash.

* The sauce will keep for several days in an airtight container in the fridge, and it can also be frozen.

Preparation time: 30 minutes Cooking time: 45–50 minutes

Snack Time
Le goûter

LA POMME · LE SAC À DOS · LES OEUFS · LE CAHIER · LA TABLE · LE CHOCOLAT

LE FOUR · LA LIMONADE · LA CASSEROLE · LES CRAYONS · LA FRAMBOISE · L'ASSIETTE

LE SANDWICH · LE GÂTEAU

LE CITRON · LES OEUFS

LA TABLE · LE SAC À DOS

LE CAHIER · LA CASSEROLE · LA POMME · LE FOUR · LE ROBINET · LE SANDWICH

LE CHOCOLAT · L'ASSIETTE · LE CITRON · LA FRAMBOISE · LA LIMONADE · LES CRAYONS

Snacking between meals is not really the done thing in France. Even French food adverts come with a slogan: *Pour être en forme, évitez de grignoter dans la journée* (to stay in shape, avoid snacking during the day). However, *le goûter* is an exception. Similar to the British afternoon tea, it's a little less formal—no cream teas with scones here. A simple sweet or savory snack around 4 p.m. lets the French *avoir la pêche* ("have the peach," or be in great form).

My first job in Paris taught me a thing or two about the way of life in the City of Light. Working for a French Scottish family, looking after two girls, gave me a great insight. They were more than happy to show me the French way of doing things, and I quickly learned that *le goûter* is an essential part of daily life, especially for French kids. Mothers, grandmothers, and nannies would be waiting at the school gates with a snack in hand or would pop by the local *boulangerie* to pick one up.

Le goûter is not just for kids, though; adults need their afternoon pick-me-up too! I love all the recipes in this chapter, but a particular favorite snack has to be a simple *pain au chocolat*—not the flaky croissant type more usually eaten for breakfast but, quite simply, a piece of bread (fresh crusty baguette works best) stuffed with a piece of good-quality chocolate (dark or milk, follow your taste buds, it doesn't really matter). This is something I came across during my time as a nanny and it's probably not the healthiest snack, but then *le goûter* is also about indulging oneself a little. And the French are the absolute masters at that . . .

Croque Madame muffins

Cheese, ham, and egg sandwich muffins

Croque Monsieur is essentially a toasted cheese and ham sandwich. Put a fried egg on top and you've got a *Croque Madame* (the egg is supposed to resemble a lady's hat). What makes the difference between a toasted cheese and ham sandwich and a *Croque Monsieur* is the cheese—in a *Croque Monsieur* it comes in the form of a creamy cheese sauce. And boy, does this make a difference!

My version of *Croque Madame* uses the bread as a muffin cup to contain the delicious cheese sauce and egg. Great as a snack, or have it with a green salad and fries, as they serve it in French cafés.

For the Mornay (cheese) sauce: **1 tbsp butter • 1 tbsp all-purpose flour • ¾ cup plus 1 tbsp milk, lukewarm • ½ tsp Dijon mustard • ½ tsp nutmeg • ¼ cup grated Gruyère or mature Comté cheese (or a strong hard cheese like Parmesan or mature Cheddar) • salt and pepper**

• 6 large slices of white bread, no crusts • 3 tbsp butter, melted • 2½ oz ham, cut into cubes or thin strips • 6 small eggs

TO MAKE THE SAUCE: Melt the butter in a pan over a medium heat. Add the flour and beat hard until you have a smooth paste. Take off the heat and leave to cool for 2 minutes, then gradually add the milk, whisking constantly. Place the pan back over a medium heat, add the mustard and nutmeg, and simmer gently for 10 minutes, whisking frequently to stop the sauce burning on the bottom of the pan. Once the sauce thickens and has the consistency of a thick tomato sauce, take it off the heat. Add the cheese (keep a little for the garnish) and taste for seasoning. If the sauce is too thick, add a little more milk. If it's lumpy, pass it through a sieve.

To assemble, preheat the oven to 350°F. Flatten the slices of bread with a rolling pin, then brush each slice on both sides with melted butter. Line a 6-cup muffin tin with the slices of bread, pressing them in with the bottom of a small glass. Divide the ham between the muffin cups followed by the eggs (if the egg seems too big, pour a little of the white away before using). Put 2 tablespoons cheese sauce on top of each egg, then sprinkle with a little cheese and pepper. Bake for 15–20 minutes, depending on how runny you like your eggs. Serve immediately.

Preparation time: 20 minutes Baking time: 15–20 minutes

Crêpes et galettes

Pancakes and buckwheat pancakes

The Americans have burgers and hot dogs; the English, sandwiches. The French? They have *crêpes* and *galettes*. Originally from Brittany, these thin pancakes have been adopted as the national snack, and tiny booths serving hot disks of doughy goodness can be found on virtually every Parisian street (or so it seems). Order a *crêpe* with a simple sprinkle of sugar, or choose from a list of fillings such as chocolate spread or *crème de marrons* (sweetened chestnut cream)—or try egg, cheese, and ham in a buckwheat pancake. If you're eating them the traditional way, they should be washed down with a glass of Breton cider. See page 78 for some filling and topping ideas.

For the crêpes: 1½ cups all-purpose flour • a pinch of sugar • a pinch of salt
• 2 eggs • about 2¼ cups milk • melted butter, for frying

For the galettes: 1½ cups buckwheat flour • a pinch of salt
• about 2½ cups water • melted butter, for frying

TO MAKE THE *CRÊPES*: Mix the flour, sugar, and salt in a bowl. Make a well in the center and crack in the eggs. Gradually mix the ingredients together, adding enough milk for the batter to have the consistency of heavy cream. Don't overmix as this will make rubbery *crêpes*. Refrigerate for a minimum of an hour, or overnight. Before using, stir the batter and add more milk if necessary to give it the consistency of heavy cream (it may have thickened on standing).

TO MAKE THE *GALETTES*: Mix the flour and salt in a bowl. Make a well in the center and gradually mix in the water, adding only enough for the batter to have the consistency of heavy cream. Don't overmix as this will make rubbery *galettes*. Refrigerate for a minimum of an hour, or overnight. Before using, whisk again and add more water if necessary.

Heat a 6–7-inch heavy *crêpe* pan and brush with some melted butter. Pour 3–4 tablespoons of the batter into the pan and quickly swirl the pan so the batter covers the whole of the inside. Cook for 1 minute, loosen around the edge with a spatula, then turn over and cook for another minute. Slide out of the pan,* then repeat to make 10–12 altogether, greasing the pan with butter in between each one.**

 * *Don't worry—the first one always tends to come out a little wrong.*
 ** *To keep the cooked* crêpes/galettes *warm: place them on a baking sheet, cover loosely with aluminum foil, and place in the oven at 250°F.*

Preparation time: 10 minutes Resting time: 1 hour–overnight Cooking time: 30 minutes

Filling and topping ideas for *crêpes* and *galettes*

To be honest, you could pretty much serve anything with a *crêpe* or *galette*, as long as it's not too liquid. Here are some ideas.

Sweet: sugar and lemon, chocolate spread, jam, crème fraîche or whipped cream with fresh fruit (especially berries), caramel spread, ice cream

Savory: cheese, ham or other cooked meats, leftover roast meat, smoked salmon, salad, tomatoes, fried egg, roasted vegetables, mushrooms

---

Crêpes avec une sauce Suzette caramelisée

Pancakes with a caramel Suzette sauce

• finely grated zest of 1 orange • juice of 2 oranges (about ⅔ cup)
• ⅓ cup orange liqueur • ½ cup sugar • 7 tbsp soft butter, cubed • 10–12 *Crêpes* (page 77)

Put the orange zest and juice into a pan with the liqueur and sugar. Reduce for 15 minutes or until you have a thick, golden syrup.* Whisk in a cube of butter at a time, taking care as the hot caramel may splatter.

Fold the warm *crêpes* into quarters and place on a serving dish. Pour the sauce over the *crêpes* and serve immediately.

* *If you prefer the traditional* crêpe Suzette *sauce, just bring the orange zest and juice, liqueur, and sugar to a boil (don't caramelize), then turn off the heat and whisk in the butter.*

Preparation time: 5 minutes Cooking time: 15 minutes

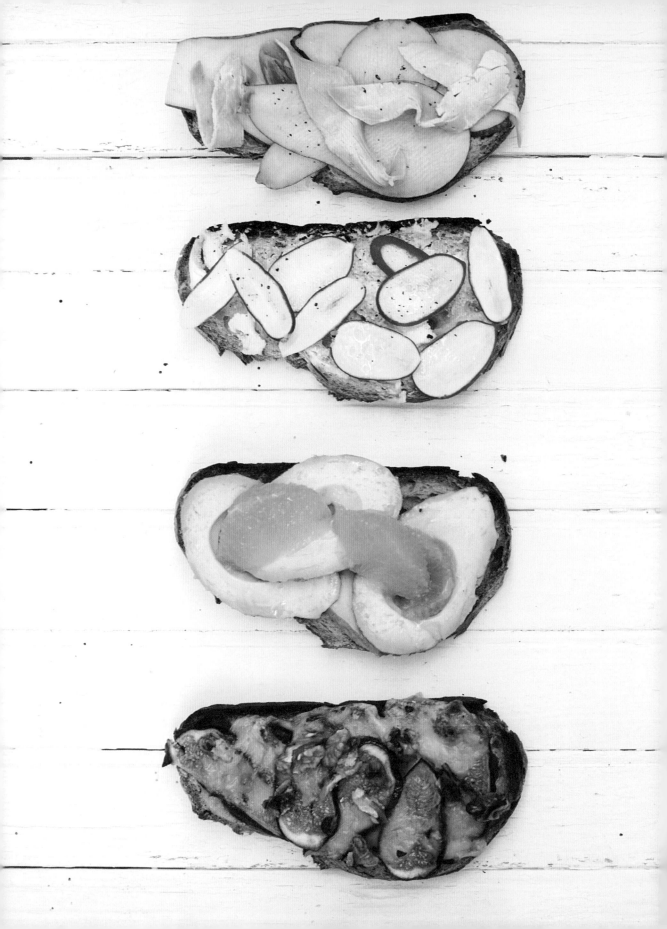

Tartines sucrées et salées

Sweet and savory open-faced sandwiches

Tartine comes from the French verb *tartiner*, meaning "to spread." You *tartine* your topping on a slice of bread or toast, making an open sandwich. Whether it's the classic butter and jam for breakfast or the after-school children's favorite of chocolate squares, *tartine* toppings should remain simple and the bread is just as important as what goes on top—if not more so. Choosing bread in a *boulangerie* can be quite overwhelming. Of course there's the classic baguette, but then there's a whole range of other breads, such as sourdough, whole wheat, and rye, and breads with nuts, figs, and other dried fruit. *Tartines* are all about enjoying the simple pleasure of a good piece of bread or toast with a topping or two.

Each topping is enough for one piece of bread or toast.

Savory toppings

Roast ham and pear

Brush the bread or toast with a little extra virgin olive oil. Thinly slice half a pear. Top the bread with the pear and some strips of roast ham.

Radish and salted butter

Spread the bread or toast with some salted butter (alternatively mix 1 tablespoon unsalted butter with some coarse sea salt). Thinly slice several radishes and place on top.

Avocado and grapefruit

Slice half an avocado. Cut out the segments from a quarter of a grapefruit. Arrange the avocado and grapefruit on the bread or toast. Sprinkle with a little salt and olive oil.

Goat's cheese, fig, and walnuts

Cut a fig into thin slices and place on the bread. Crumble some goat's cheese on top, followed by a couple of walnuts. Put under the broiler for a minute or two if you like. »»»

Sweet toppings

Caramelized apples

Butter the bread with some salted butter. Thinly slice half a small apple. Arrange the apple slices on the bread and sprinkle with sugar. Set under the broiler for a couple of minutes until caramelized, or use a blowtorch to caramelize the sugar. Works equally well with other fruit such as bananas, plums, and pears.

Strawberries, crème fraîche, and mint

Spread a generous layer of crème fraîche over the bread or toast. Top with sliced strawberries, a few leaves of mint, a sprinkle of sugar, and a little more crème fraîche.

Chocolate and olive oil

Put a chocolate bar into the freezer for 10 minutes before grating a generous handful. Brush the bread with some extra virgin olive oil and top with the grated chocolate. Put under the broiler for a couple of minutes for a melted chocolate *tartine*.

Peach and Brie

Thinly slice half a peach. Top the bread or toast with a few slices of the peach and some Brie cheese.

Chouquettes

Sugar puffs

Light, airy puffs covered with pearl sugar (coarse sugar that doesn't melt), *chouquettes* are less well known than profiteroles and éclairs, their choux-pastry cousins. *Chouquette* is derived from *chou* (cabbage), and the French use the endearing expression *mon petit chou* for their loved ones. "My little cabbage" doesn't have quite the same ring in English, though, does it? Make sure you have all your ingredients measured and ready to hand.

• ½ cup water • ½ cup milk • 7 tbsp butter, cubed • 1 tsp salt
• 1 tsp sugar • 1⅓ cups bread flour* • 4 eggs • confectioners' sugar, for dusting
• ½ cup pearl sugar (also called nibbed or hail sugar)**

Preheat the oven to 350°F. Pour the water and milk into a pan and add the butter, salt, and sugar. Place the pan on a high heat and melt the butter. Turn the heat down to low and add all of the flour. Beat hard. At this point the mixture will have the consistency of lumpy mashed potatoes. Continue beating until you have a smooth ball that pulls away from the sides of the pan without sticking.

Take the pan off the heat and continue to beat until the dough is cold enough to touch. Mix in the eggs one at a time—the batter will go lumpy when you add them, but beating continuously will smooth it out. Once all the eggs are incorporated and the mixture is smooth, put the dough into a piping bag fitted with a ¼-inch nozzle. Line several baking sheets with parchment paper, dotting a little dough in each corner to stick the paper down.

To pipe the *chouquettes*, hold the nozzle at a 90-degree angle about ¼ inch from the pan. Keep the nozzle upright and pipe a walnut-sized ball of dough, then quickly flick the nozzle sideways to stop the dough trailing. Repeat to make 20–30 *chouquettes*, with a ¾-inch gap between. If they come out too pointy, dip your finger in some water and gently pat the points down; otherwise they will burn in the oven.

Dust the *chouquettes* with confectioners' sugar and then leave for a minute before sprinkling with the pearl sugar. Repeat with a second layer of confectioners' sugar before baking for 20 minutes or until golden and crisp.

Chouquettes are best eaten straightaway, but they can be kept in an airtight container for several days. To crisp up, bake at 300°F for 5 minutes.

 * *For chocolate choux pastry, replace 3 tablespoons flour with ¼ cup unsweetened cocoa powder.*

** *Instead of pearl sugar, try finely chopped nuts mixed with a little raw cane sugar, or chocolate chips.*

Preparation time: 30 minutes Baking time: 20–30 minutes

Gougères

Cheese puffs

The savory version of *Chouquettes* (page 84). They are traditionally sprinkled with a strong cheese, like a mature Comté, but I like them topped with black sesame seeds, herbs, and spices too. These savory, salty puffs are seriously moreish. Make sure you have all your ingredients measured and ready to hand.

• ½ cup water • ½ cup milk • **7 tbsp butter**, cubed • **1 tsp salt**
• **1 tsp sugar** • a pinch of chile powder • **1⅓ cups bread flour**
• ⅔ cup grated mature hard or semi-hard cheese (e.g., Gruyère, Comté, Parmesan, or Cheddar)
• **2 tbsp finely chopped herbs**, e.g., parsley, cilantro, basil, or chives (optional) • **4 eggs**

Preheat the oven to 350°F. Pour the water and milk into a pan and add the butter, salt, sugar, and chile powder. Place the pan on a high heat and melt the butter. Turn the heat down to low and add all of the flour. Beat hard. At this point the mixture will have the consistency of lumpy mashed potatoes. Add two-thirds of the grated cheese and then the chopped herbs (if using). Continue beating until you have a smooth paste that does not stick to the sides of the pan.

Take the pan off the heat and continue to beat until the pastry is cold enough to touch. Mix in the eggs one at the time. The batter will go lumpy when you add them, but beating continuously will smooth it out. Once all the eggs are incorporated and the mixture is smooth, put the dough into a piping bag fitted with a ¼-inch nozzle. Line several baking sheets with parching paper, dotting a little dough in each corner to stick down the paper.

To pipe the *gougères*, hold the nozzle at a 90-degree angle about ¼ inch from the tray. Keep the nozzle upright and pipe a walnut-sized ball of dough, then quickly flick the nozzle sideways to stop the dough trailing. Repeat to make 20–30 *gougères*, leaving a ¾-inch gap between each one. If they come out too pointy in shape, dip your finger in some water and gently pat the points down, otherwise they will burn in the oven. Sprinkle with the rest of the grated cheese* before baking for 20 minutes or until golden and crisp.

Gougères are best eaten straightaway, but they can be kept in an airtight container for several days. To crisp up, bake at 300°F for 5 minutes.

* *Instead of the cheese topping, you could have a sprinkling of poppy, nigella, caraway, or sesame seeds, or you could top the* gougères *with both the cheese and the seeds.*

Preparation time: 30 minutes Baking time: 20 minutes

Madeleines à la crème au citron

Madeleines with lemon curd

This recipe was given to me by my friend Frankie Unsworth who, like me, studied *pâtisserie* at Le Cordon Bleu in Paris. Frankie says, "The lemon curd may take its inspiration from Melbourne's Cumulus Inc., but the basic recipe harks back to our Cordon Bleu days, when Rachel and I learned how to make this *goûter* treat. The batter can be made in advance, then baked in time for tea—madeleines should always be eaten fresh from the oven."

For the lemon curd: finely grated zest and juice of 1 lemon
• a pinch of salt • 3 tbsp sugar • 3 tbsp butter • 2 egg yolks

• 3 eggs • ⅔ cup sugar • 1½ cups all-purpose flour • 2 tsp baking powder
• finely grated zest of 1 lemon • 1½ tbsp honey • ¼ cup milk • ¾ cup plus 1 tbsp butter,
melted and cooled • 1-pt basket of raspberries • confectioners' sugar, for dusting

MAKE THE LEMON CURD: Put the lemon zest and juice, salt, sugar, and butter into a small saucepan and heat gently until the sugar and butter have melted. Remove from the heat. Whisk the egg yolks in a bowl, then add to the pan and whisk vigorously. Return the pan to a low heat and whisk constantly as the curd starts to thicken. Don't stop whisking or the eggs will curdle (if the curd starts to boil, take off the heat). Once the curd thickens and releases a bubble or two, remove from the heat, and pass the curd through a sieve into a bowl. Place plastic wrap in direct contact with the curd and refrigerate for at least an hour, preferably overnight.

Beat the eggs with the sugar until pale and frothy. Measure the flour and baking powder into a separate bowl and add the lemon zest. Mix the honey and milk with the cool butter, then add to the eggs. In two batches, fold in the flour. Cover and leave to rest in the fridge for a few hours, or overnight.

When you are ready to bake, preheat the oven to 375°F. Butter and flour a 12-shell madeleine pan. Put the lemon curd into a piping bag fitted with a small, pointed nozzle and place in the fridge.

Put a heaped tablespoon of batter into each madeleine shell and press a raspberry deep into the batter. Bake for 5 minutes, turn the oven off for 1 minute (the madeleines will get their signature peaks), then turn the oven on to 325°F and bake for another 5 minutes. Transfer the madeleines to a wire rack and leave for a few minutes until cool enough to handle. Meanwhile, wash and dry the pan, then repeat the baking as for the first batch. While the second batch is baking, pop the piping nozzle into the mound in each baked madeleine and squirt in a teaspoon's worth of lemon curd. Repeat with the second batch, then dust with confectioners' sugar and serve straightaway.

Preparation time: 40 minutes Resting time: a few hours—overnight
Cooking time: 15 minutes Baking time: 22 minutes

Quatre-quarts aux agrumes

Citrus fruit cake

Quatre-quarts is the French equivalent of pound cake. It's a recipe that most French cooks know of by heart because it's so simple to remember. As its name suggests, it has four main ingredients (flour, sugar, eggs, and butter). *C'est tout!*

• 4 eggs • 1¼ cups superfine sugar • 2 cups all-purpose flour
• a pinch of salt • finely grated zest of 1 lemon and 1 orange
• 1 tsp baking powder • 1 cup butter, melted and cooled

Preheat the oven to 350°F and butter and flour a 9-by-5-inch loaf pan. Separate the eggs. In a bowl, beat the egg whites to stiff peaks with half of the sugar. In another bowl, beat the egg yolks and the other half of the sugar until thick and pale in color.

In a separate bowl, mix the flour, salt, zest, and baking powder together.

Fold the flour mixture into the egg yolk mixture, then pour in the melted and cooled butter, stirring gently until the butter is just incorporated into the mix. Finally, carefully fold in the egg whites.

Pour the batter into the prepared pan, then bake for 35–40 minutes or until the point of a knife comes out clean when inserted in the center.

The cake is best eaten the same day, but it will keep in an airtight container for a day or two.

Preparation time: 20 minutes   Baking time: 35–40 minutes

Briochettes au dulce de leche

Dulce de leche brioche buns

The *brioche* recipe I use here is similar to *brioche vendéenne*, which is traditionally shaped as a braid for Easter and is made with crème fraîche and orange flower water.

The dough makes a great base for buns, and one of my favorite fillings is the Argentinian caramel spread *dulce de leche*. I discovered it during my first cooking job in Paris, at the cookery store La Cocotte. I used to bake *coquetines* (biscuits filled with *dulce de leche*) and other sweet treats for their tea salon and book events.

• 5 tbsp butter • 3½ tbsp milk • 1 tsp active dry yeast • 2 cups all-purpose flour • ¼ cup sugar
• a pinch of salt • 1 egg, beaten, plus beaten egg, for the egg wash • 1 heaped tbsp crème fraîche
• 1 tsp vanilla extract • 1 tsp orange flower water • ⅔ cup *dulce de leche*
• 3 small dessert apples, cored and roughly chopped, or 1 cup nuts
(e.g., almonds or hazelnuts), roughly chopped (optional)

Melt the butter in the milk. Add the yeast and stir to dissolve (the milk should be lukewarm, definitely not hot, otherwise the yeast will not work).

In a large bowl, mix together the flour, sugar, and salt. Create a well in the middle, add the milk mixture and the rest of the ingredients, and combine together until you have a soft, sticky dough. Place in a bowl, cover with plastic wrap and refrigerate overnight.

The next day, line a 10-inch springform pan (3¼–4 inches deep), or a regular cake pan, with parchment paper. Turn the dough onto a well-floured surface and knead for 5 minutes, then roll into a large rectangle (roughly 12 by 16 inches). Spread the *dulce de leche* on top, leaving a ¾-inch border, and sprinkle over the chopped apples or nuts (if using). Roll up the dough to make a long sausage and cut into six equal pieces. Place each piece, swirl-side up, into the prepared pan and brush with egg wash. Cover and leave to rise in a warm place for 2 hours or until doubled in size.

Preheat the oven to 325°F. Egg wash the buns a second time and then bake for 30–40 minutes or until golden brown. If the briochettes start browning too much, cover with some aluminum foil. Remove from the oven and transfer to a wire rack to cool. Best eaten warm, or on the same day.

Preparation time: 30 minutes
Resting time: overnight, plus a couple of hours
Baking time: 30–40 minutes

Pain perdu avec compote de cerises et basilic

French toast with cherry and basil compote

Pain perdu means "lost bread," but this dish finds its way to my stomach quite easily. I've topped it with my favorite compote, but you can eat it just as it comes, without any topping at all.

*For the compote:** 1 lb frozen pitted cherries • 1½ cups confectioners' sugar
• a bunch of basil (about ⅔ oz)

• 1 egg • 1 cup milk • 1 tbsp sugar
• 4 slices of *brioche* or sandwich bread • 1 tbsp butter

TO MAKE THE COMPOTE: Place all the ingredients in a pot and simmer uncovered for 15 minutes. Stir occasionally during this time to help dissolve the sugar.

Meanwhile, whisk the egg, milk, and sugar together in a dish. Place the *brioche* in the egg mixture and soak for a minute on each side. Heat the butter in a large frying pan on a medium heat. Add the *brioche* and cook for 2–3 minutes or until golden, then flip the slices over and cook the other side.

Remove the basil from the compote. Serve the *pain perdu* straight from the pan, with the warm compote spooned over and around.

* *The compote can be made in advance and kept for several days in an airtight container in the fridge, ready to be reheated when you want it.*

Other topping ideas

• sliced banana and chocolate sauce

• crispy bacon and maple syrup

• fresh berries and a scoop of ice cream

• salted caramel sauce (see page 249)

Preparation time: 10 minutes   Cooking time: 25 minutes

Fromage frais

Fresh cheese

Fromage frais has a smooth, creamy taste and a subtle acidic note, making it less smelly socks and more freshly washed white linen. Of course, an additional plus is that it's low in fat and cholesterol, but that doesn't mean it's low in taste.

- 2 qt 2-percent or skimmed milk, preferably organic but not UHT or homogenized
- ½ cup plain live or probiotic yogurt, preferably organic • juice of 1 lemon (6 tbsp)
- a pinch of salt or sugar • 2 tbsp heavy cream (optional)

Pour the milk into a large pot. Heat very slowly, stirring gently, until it starts to steam and little bubbles form around the edge (it should not boil at any point). This should take about 20 minutes.

Allow to cool for a couple of minutes before stirring in the yogurt and lemon juice. Leave to sit undisturbed for a further 10 minutes. Return the pot to the heat and bring the milk to a boil. Once it separates into curds (the solids) and whey (the liquid), remove from the heat.

Line a fine-meshed sieve with cheesecloth or a clean tea towel. Place the sieve over a bowl and pour in the separated milk. Scrunch the cloth tightly immediately above the cheese, like making a money bag, and twist to squeeze out any excess liquid. Now tie the corners of the cloth together to form a hanging pouch and thread a wooden spoon through the loop. Hang the cheese over a large bowl or jug (don't let it sit on the bottom), and refrigerate for 30 minutes or overnight. The longer the cheese hangs, the more the liquid will drip away and the drier the cheese will become.

To serve, twist the cloth as before to squeeze out any excess liquid, then remove the cheese from the cloth and season with salt or sugar. Serve as it comes for a firm version, or beat in a couple of tablespoons of heavy cream for a smoother, creamier cheese.

Serving ideas

Spread the cheese over a slice of toasted *brioche* or bread, then just let your imagination and taste buds get creative to sweeten or spice it up. These are some of my favorite flavorings.

Sweet: a drizzle of honey or maple syrup or a sprinkling of sugar can be quite sufficient. Or serve with fresh or stewed fruit (berries are especially good). For a crunch factor, try nuts or granola.

Savory: cracked black pepper, a pinch of chile, or freshly chopped herbs (chives, parsley, etc.)

Preparation time: 10 minutes   Cooking time: 25 minutes
Resting time: 30 minutes–overnight

LE SOLEIL

LE SAUCISSON SEC

LA BAGUETTE

L'HERBE

LES VERRES

UNE BOUTEILLE DE VIN

LA PLUIE

LES FROMAGES

LES RAISINS

LE THERMOS

LES SERVIETTES

LA COUVERTURE

LE PANIER

LE THERMOS

LA PLUIE

L'ARBRE

LE SAUCISSON SEC

LES VERRES

L'HERBE

Summer Picnics

Pique-niques d'été

LE TIRE BOUCHON

LA COUVERTURE

LE SOLEIL

UNE BOUTEILLE DE VIN

LES ABEILLES

LA BAGUETTE

LES FROMAGES

LE PANIER

LES RAISINS

LES FLEURS

In the mid-nineteenth century, Édouard Manet and Claude Monet both painted picnic scenes, *Le déjeuner sur l'herbe* ("lunch on the grass"). Manet's painting (which in turn inspired Monet) caused quite a stir. The picnic is set in a luscious green opening in a forest. A naked woman sits with two fully dressed men who are so deep in conversation that they don't seem at all distracted by their nude companion. Fruits and bread seem to have spilled out of their picnic basket, but none of the guests seems to be too bothered about eating. That is certainly not the case with the Parisian picnics I've been to—the food is the star of the show!

In Paris, as soon as spring sunshine begins to warm the city and cold, gray winter weather is chased away, you'll find Parisians heading to any green or watery spot. Along the Seine or the canal, on the Champ de Mars under the Eiffel Tower and in many other Parisian parks, people congregate with their baguettes, bottles of wine, and other picnic paraphernalia.

My favorite park in Paris has to be the Parc des Buttes Chaumont in the 19th arrondissement. Unlike the Jardin du Luxembourg or Parc Monceau, this park is very green, with plenty of grass that you can actually sit on (whereas some Parisian parks ban sitting on the grass), lots of trees, and a beautiful view over Paris. During the summer months it becomes my second home, especially since I'm lucky enough to live next door. Picnics are *the* summer social gatherings among my friends, as we all have typical tiny Parisian apartments that make entertaining for lots of people impossible. Plus there's really not much to organizing a picnic— just ask everyone to bring something along and you're sorted. This chapter is full of my personal picnic favorites—I hope you enjoy them.

Quiche Lorraine

Bacon and egg tart

Quiche Lorraine should only be pastry, cream, eggs, and bacon. No cheese, no onions, nor any extra flavors. *Quiche* originates from Lorraine, the region of France that borders Germany. The word *quiche* comes from the German word *Kuchen*, meaning "cake."

A *quiche* is basically a savory custard tart. Add bacon and you have *quiche Lorraine*; add some Gruyère cheese and you have *quiche Vosgienne*. Add whatever filling you fancy—see my suggestions below—and you'll have *quiche à la [your name]*!

• 6 tbsp soft butter • 1 tsp sugar • a pinch of salt
• 1⅓ cups all-purpose flour • 2 eggs, separated • ice-cold water

For the filling: 5 oz lardons or cubes of smoked bacon* • 4 eggs plus 2 egg yolks
• 1¼ cups crème fraîche or heavy cream • 1 tsp salt • pepper

Using a wooden spoon,** beat together the butter, sugar, and salt until soft and creamy. Mix in the flour followed by the egg yolks and 2 tablespoons ice-cold water. Mix and bring together to make a smooth ball, adding a little more water if the pastry is too crumbly (only knead as much as necessary to bring the dough together). Wrap the dough in plastic wrap and refrigerate for a minimum of an hour (best overnight).

Remove the pastry from the fridge 30 minutes before using. Roll out the pastry between two sheets of parchment paper until it is ¼ inch thick, and use to line a 10-inch quiche pan that is at least 1¼ inches deep. Brush the pastry base with egg white. Refrigerate while preparing the filling.

Preheat the oven to 350°F.

TO MAKE THE FILLING: Fry the lardons in a nonstick frying pan until golden brown, then lift out with a slotted spoon and leave to cool on paper towels. Meanwhile, lightly beat the eggs and egg yolks in a bowl, add the crème fraîche and seasoning, and continue to beat until mixed together. Scatter the lardons in the pastry shell and then pour in the egg mix. Bake for 30–45 minutes or until the filling is golden brown and set. Serve warm or cold.

* *Alternative fillings: roasted vegetables • asparagus and smoked salmon • cherry tomatoes, cubes of Cheddar cheese, and thyme leaves • softened mushrooms and leeks*

** *You can use a food processor to make the pastry, but be careful not to overmix.*

Preparation time: 30 minutes   Resting time: 1 hour–overnight
Baking time: 30–45 minutes

Pissaladière

Anchovy, onion, and black olive tart

A lot of people think that the Provençal *pissaladière* is the French version of the classic Italian pizza. In fact, *pissaladière* gets its name from *pissala*, a salty fish paste originally used to flavor the dish. Nowadays, the pizza-esque base is topped with anchovies instead of the fish paste, together with slowly cooked onions and black olives.

• 1 tsp active dry yeast • ⅓ cup warm water • a pinch of sugar
• 1¼ cups bread flour • ½ tsp salt • ½ tsp dried rosemary
• 1 tbsp olive oil, plus extra for brushing

For the topping: 1 lb large onions, thinly sliced • 8 anchovies,* drained of oil
• 1 tbsp olive oil, plus extra for drizzling • a pinch of sugar
• finely grated zest of 1 orange (optional) • 10 black olives, pitted

Dissolve the yeast in the warm water with the sugar. Combine the rest of the dry ingredients in a bowl, pour in the dissolved yeast and the olive oil, and mix to form a dough. Turn the dough onto a lightly floured surface and knead until silky smooth and fairly elastic (a good 5 minutes).

Brush a baking sheet with olive oil. Roll out the dough until it is ⅛ inch thick (like a thin pizza and any shape you want), then place it on the pan, pushing it a little way up the sides. Brush with olive oil, cover with a damp tea towel, and leave to rise in a warm place for 30 minutes.

MEANWHILE, MAKE THE TOPPING: Gently fry the onions and 2 of the anchovies in the 1 tablespoon olive oil for 30–40 minutes. Once the onions are soft and have a marmalade consistency, mix in the sugar and orange zest (if using). Leave to cool for 10 minutes.

Preheat the oven to 400°F. Spread the onions over the dough, followed by the remaining anchovies.** Drizzle some olive oil on top and bake for 20–25 minutes or until the base is golden. Take out of the oven and put the olives on top. Serve warm or cold.

* *The anchovies I buy are the luxury kind that are kept in good olive oil. They are less salty than the canned fillets you get at the supermarket. If the ones you buy are super-salty, they should be rinsed carefully and dried on paper towels.*

** *If you prefer your anchovies juicy rather than crisp, add them with the olives at the end (olives tend to shrivel up and burn if baked).*

Preparation time: 30 minutes Resting time: 30 minutes
Cooking time: about 1 hour

Tarte flambée

Onion and crème fraîche tart

Provence has *pissaladière*, while in Alsace they have *tarte flambée*, a pizza-style base topped with crème fraîche, lardons, and onions—popular ingredients in Alsatian cuisine.

Gluten-free is a concept that hasn't quite caught on in the land of baguettes, and it can be frustrating for anyone on a gluten-free diet who wants to try delicious French pastries and bread, so here I've replaced the regular wheat base with chestnut flour and tapioca starch. This means no kneading is required—just mix the ingredients together to form a ball.

- 1⅓ cups chestnut flour* • 1¼ cups tapioca starch • 1 tsp guar gum** • 1½ tsp baking powder
- ½ tsp salt • 1 tbsp soft light brown sugar • 1 tsp active dry yeast • ½ tsp sugar
- ¾ cups plus 1 tbsp warm water • 4 tbsp crème fraîche • 2 red onions, thinly sliced
- 3½ oz lardons or cubes of smoked bacon • 4 sprigs of thyme, leaves only

Mix together the flour, tapioca starch, guar gum, baking powder, salt, and sugar in a large bowl. Make a well in the middle. Dissolve the yeast and sugar in the warm water. When the yeast begins to foam, pour it into the well and mix everything together to form a ball. Roll out the dough between two pieces of parchment paper until ¼ inch thick, then place in a baking pan that is large enough for the pastry to sit flat. (The shape doesn't really matter, it's the ¼-inch thickness that's important.) Remove the top layer of paper and trim off any excess paper from around the bottom edges.

Preheat the oven to 400°F and place a large baking sheet in the oven to get hot.

Spread the crème fraîche over the dough, then sprinkle the onions, lardons, and thyme leaves on top. Slide the baking pan onto the hot baking sheet and bake for 20—30 minutes or until the edges are crisp. The tart is traditionally eaten warm, but it's great cold too.

* Chestnut flour can be bought in health food shops and online. For tapioca starch, try your supermarket or a Chinese grocery store.

** Guar gum is a very powerful thickening agent made from guar beans. You can find it in powdered form online and in health food shops.

Alternative idea

- *For a sweet topping, replace the onions and lardons with thinly sliced apples and a sprinkle of ground cinnamon and brown sugar.*

Preparation time: 30 minutes Baking time: 20—30 minutes

Cake au saucisson sec avec pistaches et prunes

Cured sausage, pistachio, and prune cake

A cake with cured sausage, pistachio, and prunes? *Pourquoi pas?* The French have been making savory cakes for quite a while. They appear in boulangeries and with a side salad on lunch menus in chic cafés, and they're most likely to appear at a picnic (my first encounter). They are super-simple to make and can be adapted to use whatever leftovers you have in your fridge—roasted vegetables, cold meats, cheese. Just follow the basic batter recipe and get creative with the fillings.

• 2 cups all-purpose flour • 1 tbsp baking powder • 5 oz cured French sausage or salami, finely chopped • ¾ cup pistachios, roughly chopped • ⅔ cup prunes, roughly chopped • 4 eggs • ¼ cup milk • ⅔ cup olive oil • ¼ cup plain yogurt • 1 tsp salt • pepper

Preheat the oven to 350°F and line a 1-pound loaf pan with parchment paper. In a bowl, mix together the flour, baking powder, sausage, pistachios, and prunes. In a separate bowl, whisk the eggs until thick and pale in color. Gradually whisk in the milk, oil, and yogurt, then add the salt, season with pepper, and fold in the flour mixture bit by bit. Try not to overbeat (it's better to undermix).*

Pour the batter into the prepared pan. Bake for 30–40 minutes or until a metal skewer inserted in the center of the cake comes out clean. Leave to cool in the pan.

Pourquoi?

The more the batter is beaten when the flour is added, the more the gluten gets developed. For cakes and pastries, too much gluten is not desirable (unlike for bread) as it makes the end result tough. To prevent overbeating when adding the flour, you may find it easier to use a rubber spatula rather than a whisk.

Preparation time: 20 minutes Baking time: 30–40 minutes

Salade de carrottes râpées et rémoulade de céleri-rave et pommes

Carrot salad and Celeriac and apple salad

Carrot and celeriac salads are staples on many lunch menus. There's not much to the recipes, just the main ingredient and a vinaigrette, and therein lies the pleasure. So simple that they can be effortlessly whipped up for a picnic in a matter of minutes.

For the carrot salad: **8 carrots, grated*** • **½ bunch of parsley, finely chopped**
• **5 tbsp sunflower oil** • **juice of ½ lemon** • **salt and pepper**

For the celeriac and apple salad: **8 oz celeriac, grated*** • **1 dessert apple, peeled and grated***
• **5 tbsp sunflower oil** • **2 tbsp white wine vinegar**
• **1 heaped tsp grainy mustard** • **a pinch of sugar** • **salt and pepper**

TO MAKE THE CARROT SALAD: Put the carrots and parsley into a bowl. Make a vinaigrette by mixing together the oil and lemon juice and seasoning with salt and pepper. Pour the vinaigrette over the carrots and toss everything together. Taste for seasoning.**

TO MAKE THE CELERIAC AND APPLE SALAD: Put the celeriac and apple into a bowl. Make a vinaigrette by mixing together the oil, wine vinegar, mustard, and sugar. Season with salt and pepper. Pour the vinaigrette over the celeriac and apple and toss everything together. Taste for seasoning.**

* *If you have a grating attachment on your food processor to make fine little matchsticks, use this rather than a traditional grater. A bit more work, but the texture of the matchsticks creates a crunchier salad.*

** *Both salads are best eaten on the day you make them (celeriac and apple has a tendency to discolor, even with the dressing). Keep them in separate airtight containers in the fridge until it's time to take them to the picnic.*

Preparation time: 20 minutes (for both salads)

"Choosing bread in a boulangerie can be quite overwhelming. Of course, there's the classic baguette but there's also a whole range of other breads, such as sourdough, whole wheat and rye, and breads with nuts, figs, and other dried fruit."

Pain brié

Olive bread

This recipe was given to me by Gontran Cherrier, who comes from a family of bakers going back three generations. He has several cookbooks under his belt and runs a Parisian bakery, so when it comes to bread he certainly knows what he's talking about. His *pain brié* is typical of the Normandy region and is simple to make. I baked it for a picnic and it must have been good—by the time I wanted to try some, it was all gone.

• 1 tsp active dry yeast • 4 tbsp warm water • ⅔ cup all-purpose flour • a generous pinch of salt
• 2 tbsp soft butter • 10 oz fermented dough*

For the filling: ⅓ cup green olives, pitted • ⅓ cup black olives, pitted
• 1 tsp finely chopped rosemary (optional) • 4 tsp olive oil

Dissolve the yeast in the warm water. Mix the flour and salt together in a large bowl. Add the dissolved yeast, butter, and fermented dough and bring together to form a ball. Turn the ball out onto a floured surface and knead for 15 minutes or until the dough becomes smooth. Cover with a damp tea towel and leave to rise in a warm place for 30 minutes.

TO MAKE THE FILLING: Mix together the olives and rosemary (if using) with the olive oil.

Roll out the dough on a floured surface to a rectangle that is about ⅜ inch thick and slightly larger than a sheet of computer paper. Spread the olive mixture on top. Roll up the dough lengthwise to form a large sausage, then place join-side down on a piece of parchment paper. Using a sharp knife, cut deep slits in the dough to reveal the layers of olives (but don't cut all the way down to the bottom). Cover again with a damp tea towel and leave to rise in a warm place for an hour or until doubled in size.

Preheat the oven to 475°F** with a baking sheet in the middle and a roasting pan at the bottom. Once the oven is hot, slide the bread on to the hot baking sheet (keeping it on the paper) and pour a glass of water into the roasting pan. Bake the loaf for 5 minutes, then reduce the temperature to 400°F and bake for another 20–25 minutes. Transfer to a wire rack and serve warm or cold.

* *For the fermented dough, ask your baker, or make it yourself the night before. Mix 2 teaspoons active dry yeast with ½ cup warm water. Stir until dissolved. Mix 1½ cups all-purpose flour with 2 generous pinches of salt. Pour in the dissolved yeast and mix together. Knead until it forms a smooth ball (it will be sticky at the beginning), place in a bowl, and cover with plastic wrap. Leave in a warm place for 1 hour, then refrigerate overnight.*

** *Convection ovens can dry out the bread, so use the regular setting for this loaf if you can.*

Preparation time: 30 minutes Resting time: several hours,
plus overnight Baking time: 25–30 minutes

Clafoutis—versions sucré et salé

Sweet and savory clafoutis

Clafoutis originally came from the Limousin. Baked fruit in a simple batter of eggs, sugar, ground almonds, and flour, it's the kind of dessert your French *grand-mère* would make if you had one. Traditionally whole cherries are used, but you can use whatever fruit you have. You can even get away with canned fruit, as long as you drain it well.

The French have recently taken to transforming dessert recipes into savory ones. Replace the fruit with cheese and tomatoes, leave out the sugar, and *voilà*—a savory *clafoutis*.

• 4 eggs • ¾ cup sugar • a pinch of salt • scant ½ cup ground almonds*
• 2 tbsp all-purpose flour • 7 tbsp crème fraîche • 7 tbsp milk
• 12 oz cherries, pitted, or any soft fruit or berries of your choice (or even chocolate chunks)

Preheat the oven to 350°F and butter and flour a 7½-by-4-inch baking dish or pan.** Whisk the eggs with the sugar and salt until pale yellow and thick. Sift and fold in the ground almonds and flour, then stir in the crème fraîche and milk. Scatter the cherries in the prepared dish, spreading them out evenly. Pour the batter over the cherries and bake for 30–40 minutes or until golden brown and set. Serve warm or cold.

Savory clafoutis

Make as for the sweet *clafoutis* but omit the sugar, replacing the cherries with 3½ oz mature cheese (e.g., Gruyère, mature Comté, Cheddar, or goat's cheese), chopped into large cubes; ½ cup cherry tomatoes; and ⅓ cup black olives, pitted. You could also flavor the batter with chopped herbs, such as basil, parsley, or thyme, and use leftover roasted vegetables as an alternative to the cheese and tomatoes.

 * *Almonds can be replaced with different ground nuts, such as hazelnuts or pistachios.*

** *Or make individual* clafoutis*: butter and flour 6–8 ramekins (roughly 3¼ inches in diameter and 1½ inches deep). Divide the cherries and batter between the ramekins and bake for 15–20 minutes. You can turn them out for serving if you like.*

Preparation time: 15 minutes Baking time: 30–40 minutes

Fougasse aux romarin, lavande et fromage du chèvre

Rosemary, lavender, and goat's cheese bread

The word *fougasse* stems from the ancient Roman *panis focacius*, which is probably why the bread is so similar to the Italian *focaccia*. Unlike the Italians, however, the French stretch and slice their loaf into a leaf shape. This isn't just for aesthetic reasons—the slashes increase the surface area of the bread, ensuring a crisper, faster-cooking loaf.

The bread makes a great base for any topping you fancy: leftover roasted vegetables, cheese, fruit, herbs—the possibilities are endless.

> • 2 tsp active dry yeast • 1 cup lukewarm water • 3 cups bread flour
> • 1½ tsp salt, plus extra for sprinkling • 1 tsp dried rosemary
> • ½ tsp dried lavender • 2 tbsp olive oil, plus extra for brushing
> • 3 oz hard goat's cheese, cut into small cubes

Mix the yeast with the warm water, stirring until the yeast has completely dissolved. Mix the flour, salt, rosemary, and lavender in a bowl. Pour in the dissolved yeast and the olive oil and mix to form a dough. Turn the dough onto a lightly floured surface and knead until it forms a smooth, sticky ball (don't add too much flour as it's better sticky). Cover with plastic wrap and leave to rise in a warm place for an hour, then put in the fridge overnight.

The following day, turn the dough onto a floured surface and knead for 5 minutes or until it forms a smooth ball again, then cover with a damp tea towel and leave to rise in a warm place for 30 minutes.

Roll out the dough to a large rectangle and then cut the rectangle diagonally into two triangles. Make a large cut down the middle of each triangle without cutting all the way through the dough, starting a little way in from the short edge and stopping before the opposite corner. Make three small slashes on each side of the cut, then use your fingers to gently open out the slashes to look like the veins of a leaf. Place each triangle on a piece of parchment paper and push the cubes of cheese randomly into the dough. Cover with a damp tea towel and leave to rise in a warm place for an hour or until doubled in size.

Preheat the oven to 475°F and put a baking sheet in the oven to get hot. Brush the bread with olive oil and sprinkle with a couple of pinches of salt. Once the oven is hot, place the bread on the hot baking sheet and bake for 5 minutes, then reduce the temperature to 400°F and bake for another 12–15 minutes or until the bread is golden brown. Best eaten warm.

Preparation time: 30 minutes Resting time: overnight, plus 2 hours
Baking time: 17–20 minutes

Crème Vichyssoise au chou-fleur glacé

Iced cauliflower and potato soup

Depending who you believe, Vichyssoise is either a French or an American invention. Nobody can really say for sure. One story claims that the French chef Louis Diat created it in 1914 for the Ritz–Carlton Hotel in New York City. He grew up not far from the French spa town of Vichy, which is why he named the soup Vichyssoise.

The traditional recipe calls for leeks and potatoes, but I have swapped the leeks for cauliflower, which makes a milder-tasting soup. Make it the day before serving so that it has enough time to chill, then all you need do before the picnic is pop it into a thermos.

- 1 small head of cauliflower (1¼ lb), chopped into florets – you can use some of the stalks
- 8 oz potatoes, cut into large chunks • 1 onion, chopped • 2 tbsp butter
- 5 cups hot chicken or vegetable stock • 2½ cups milk
- 7 tbsp crème fraîche, plus a little extra for serving • salt and white pepper
- a handful of chopped chives

Gently fry the vegetables in the butter for 5 minutes or until the onion is soft but not golden. Add the hot stock and simmer for 20 minutes or until the potatoes and cauliflower are soft. Leave to cool slightly before stirring in the milk and crème fraîche, then whizz in a blender until smooth and season with salt and pepper.

Refrigerate the soup until cold for at least 4 hours, preferably overnight. Taste for seasoning before serving extra cold, garnished with a dollop of crème fraîche and some chopped chives.

Preparation time: 30 minutes Cooking time: 25 minutes
Chilling time: 4 hours–overnight

Cervelles de canut

Fresh cheese with shallots and red wine

Literally translated, *cervelles de canut* means "silk worker's brains." Fear not—no cannibalism, nor even carnivorism, is committed here. The recipe originated in Lyon, which was made the capital of French silk production by Louis XI in 1466. It is thought that by the nineteenth century the silk workers were treated with such disdain by high society in the city that they named this simple dish after them. This is delicious with fresh bread and raw vegetables like carrot sticks, peppers, and radishes.

• 8 oz *fromage frais* (to make your own, see page 96) or cottage cheese
• 3½ tbsp crème fraîche • 1 tbsp red wine vinegar • 1 small shallot, finely chopped
• ½ clove of garlic, crushed to a paste • ½ tsp sugar
• 4 tbsp finely chopped chives • salt and pepper

Drain any excess liquid from the cheese. Mix all the ingredients together in a bowl, saving some of the chives for the garnish, and taste for seasoning. Cover the bowl and refrigerate the cheese for 2 hours.*

Sprinkle the cheese with chives and serve chilled.

* *Can be kept in an airtight container in the fridge for several days.*

Preparation time: 10 minutes Chilling time: 2 hours

LE THON — LE COCKTAIL — LES PISTACHES — LA MENTHE — LE CÈPE — LE RADIS

LES OIGNONS FRAIS — L'HUITRE — LES CHANTERELLES — LA SALADE — L'AIL — LE PASTIS

LES OLIVES

LES CORNICHONS

UNE COUPE DE CHAMPAGNE

Aperitifs

Apéros

LE COCKTAIL

LE CÈPE

LES PISTACHES

LE CONCOMBRE — LA SALADE — LE PASTIS — LES OLIVES — LE THON

LES CORNICHONS — LES OIGNONS FRAIS — L'HUITRE — LA RÂPE — L'AIL — LA MENTHE

"*La bonne cuisine est la base du véritable bonheur*" (Good food is the foundation of true happiness) is what the famous French chef Auguste Escoffier said, and I couldn't agree more. And what more pleasurable way to kick off an evening than with a glass of something red, white, or bubbly and a delicious nibble or two? *L'heure de l'apéro* could be considered the French version of the cocktail hour, except that there are no chips and dips on the menu, but instead you might find a selection of charcuterie (cured meats) served with some crunchy cornichons (little gherkins).

Like many traditions in France, *l'heure de l'apéro* is considered a perfect opportunity to indulge oneself, to take a moment after a hard day at work to unwind. The practice came from the nineteeth-century French custom of a *coup d'avant* (shot before). This was usually a shot of vermouth, and only served to men. Vermouth (an essential ingredient for a dry martini) was created in 1813 by herbalist Joseph Noilly, who claimed vermouth had health benefits (most aperitifs of the time made this claim). The manufacturing process has hardly changed. Grapes from Marseillan are matured in oak casks and subsequently blended with a secret mix of spices and herbs.

Another old-school favorite is pastis, an anise-flavored liqueur that is mixed with water.

Although Paris in the last couple of years has seen the rise of cocktails, the French still prefer to keep it simple. The closest the French get to a cocktail would be a Kir (a splash of crème de cassis with white wine) or Kir royal (crème de cassis with Champagne).

No matter what drinks and nibbles you decide to serve, I think the most important part is taking the time to slow down and relax. And that is most certainly a health benefit in today's crazy, hectic world.

Pâté de foie de lapin

Rabbit liver pâté

It's funny how some things you couldn't stand eating as a kid you start to love when you're a grown-up. Liver used to be like that for me. My mother would try to find creative ways of disguising it, but I could smell liver a mile off. This all changed when I took an intensive two-week cookery course and discovered that livers can be delicious, especially when made into a pâté. The trick is not to overcook them.

• 7 tbsp salted butter • 1 shallot, thinly sliced • 2 cloves of garlic, pounded flat
• 2 bay leaves • 2 sprigs of thyme • 7 oz rabbit livers,* trimmed and cleaned
• 1 tbsp Cognac • 1 small anchovy fillet • ½ tsp pepper • salt (if necessary)

For the clarified butter: ¾ cup unsalted butter

Melt 2 tablespoons of the salted butter in a large pan and add the shallot, garlic, bay leaves, and thyme. Cook until the shallot is softened but not brown. Add the livers and Cognac and cook for about 2 minutes on each side or until the livers are browned on the outside but still pink in the middle. Leave to cool for 5 minutes. Remove the bay leaves and thyme and then whizz the livers in a blender with the anchovy and the rest of the salted butter. Add the pepper and check for seasoning. Divide the pâté between four ramekins (about 2½ inches in diameter and 1½ inches deep)** and smooth the tops.

TO MAKE THE CLARIFIED BUTTER: Melt the unsalted butter in a saucepan and bring to a boil. Be careful, as it may splatter. Take off the heat and leave to stand for a few minutes, then remove the crusty white layer from the top. Underneath the crust will be the clear (clarified) butter. Pour this clear butter over the pâté in the ramekins, and discard the milky liquid at the bottom. Wrap the ramekins in plastic wrap and refrigerate for a minimum of 4 hours (or overnight) before serving. The pâté will keep refrigerated for up to a week or frozen for up to 2 months.

* The livers from farmed rabbits are mild in flavor, like chicken livers (which you can also use for this recipe). Wild rabbit livers are strong tasting and will need soaking in milk overnight before use, so that they lose some of their gamey flavor.

** Or make 1 large pâté in a 1-pound loaf pan.

Preparation time: 20 minutes Cooking time: 15 minutes
Chilling time: 4 hours–overnight

Terrine forestière

Wild mushroom terrine

When I was a child, I used to go mushroom hunting with my parents. This was long before foraging became fashionable with Michelin-starred restaurants. Looking for chanterelles, *cèpes, trompettes de la mort*, and many other forest fungi was a bit of a bore for my brother and me, and we would always hope for a rainy day (although a light drizzle wouldn't put my parents off). Needless to say, I don't do much foraging now that I live in Paris, although I like to think that going to the Parisian flea markets could be classified as urban foraging.

> • 1 lb mixed wild mushrooms • 4 tbsp butter • 2 shallots, finely chopped
> • 2 cloves of garlic, crushed to a paste • 4 eggs • 1 cup crème fraîche
> • 2 tsp Dijon mustard • a pinch of nutmeg
> • 2 tbsp chopped parsley • salt and pepper

Preheat the oven to 325°F and line two 8-ounce mini loaf pans* with parchment paper.

Clean the mushrooms carefully with paper towels or a brush, then roughly chop any that are large to make them all about the same size. Melt the butter in a large frying pan and add the shallots and garlic. Once the shallots begin to brown, add the mushrooms and fry for a good 10 minutes until they have released all their juices (if the pan is too small for them all in one go, fry in batches).

Meanwhile, beat the eggs in a bowl with the crème fraîche and mustard. Add the nutmeg and parsley and season with salt and pepper.

Remove the cooked mushroom mixture from the pan with a slotted spoon (to drain off any liquid) and divide between the prepared pans. Pour the crème fraîche mix over the mushrooms and bake for about 15 minutes or until set. Leave to cool slightly before cutting. Best served at room temperature.

Or make one large terrine in a 1-pound loaf pan and bake for about 30 minutes or until set.

Preparation time: 20 minutes Cooking time: 15 minutes

Rillettes au porc

Coarse pork pâté

Rillettes are almost always found sitting on a platter of *charcuterie*, but you won't find many people making them at home. They're the kind of thing usually bought ready-made from the supermarket or butcher. The best ones are made from fatty meats, like belly pork, goose, or duck, which are slowly roasted to allow the fat to melt. Everything is then blended to make a coarse pâté, a little seasoning is added, and that's it.

• 2 lb boned pork belly with skin* • 2 bay leaves
• 1 sprig of rosemary • 2 sprigs of thyme • salt and pepper

Preheat the oven to 275°F. Chop the pork into large pieces and place in a large baking sheet with the bay leaves, rosemary, and thyme. Cover the baking sheet with aluminum foil and cook for 3 hours, stirring halfway.

Remove the baking sheet from the oven and leave the pork to cool.

Peel the skin** off the pork. Discard the bay, rosemary, and thyme and put the meat into a blender with any fat from the pan. Whizz to a rough paste and season with salt and pepper. Transfer to a serving dish and serve at room temperature.

The *rillettes* will keep in an airtight container in the fridge for 3–4 days (the fat will harden when chilled, and the *rillettes* will need to be broken up with a fork before serving).

 * *You can replace the pork belly with boned duck legs.*

** *I put the skin under a very hot broiler for a couple of minutes to make crackling, then I cut it into small bits and season with salt before serving.*

Preparation time: 30 minutes Cooking time: 3 hours

Rouleaux de salade Niçoise

Salad Niçoise wraps

Trying to find out what an authentic *salade niçoise* should be made of is like solving a cryptic puzzle. Tuna or no tuna? Cooked vegetables or not? After an extensive survey among my foodie and French friends, I came to the conclusion that as long as it contains ingredients you would find in the vicinity of the Provençal town of Nice, then you can more or less call it a *salade niçoise*.

For the vinaigrette: 2 tbsp red wine vinegar • 4 tbsp extra virgin olive oil
• ¼ clove of garlic, crushed to a paste • juice of ½ lemon • a pinch of sugar • salt and pepper

• a pinch each of salt and sugar • 12 green beans, topped and tailed • 1 Little Gem lettuce
• 1 red Belgian endive • 12 anchovies,* drained and boned
• 12 black olives (preferably from Nice), pitted and sliced
• 6 cherry tomatoes, quartered or halved depending on size • 6 radishes, thinly sliced
• 1 green onion, thinly sliced • 2 hard-boiled eggs, peeled and each cut into 6 wedges
• 2 tbsp capers, finely chopped

TO MAKE THE VINAIGRETTE: Whisk all the ingredients together in a bowl. Taste for seasoning.

Bring a large pot of water to a boil. Add the salt and sugar followed by the green beans. Blanch for 2 minutes, then drain and rinse under cold running water.

Separate the lettuce and endive into individual leaves—you will need 12 leaves in total. Divide the remaining ingredients between the leaves, halving the beans if they are long (they should be slightly shorter than the length of the leaves). Drizzle some vinaigrette on top and serve the rest in a small bowl.

* *I prefer using the plump Provençal anchovies that are preserved in olive oil. These tend to be less salty than canned anchovy fillets, which need to be carefully rinsed and dried on paper towels before use.*

Additional ingredients

• *boiled small potatoes, halved or quartered*

• *corn*

• *tuna—season a 7-oz piece of raw tuna (preferably yellowfin) and sear in a smoking-hot pan with a little olive oil for a minute on each side, then cut into thin slices.*

Preparation time: 20 minutes Cooking time: 5 minutes

Palmiers et sacristains salés

Elephant ears and puff pastry twists

I remember having to make puff pastry at cookery school during a really hot summer. Our air-conditioning was broken and the kitchen was hot from the previous class, so my pastry and I were both melting in the heat. Not ideal! The pastry had to go into the fridge numerous times before I could finish making it, and I wished I could have got into the fridge myself.

Not wanting to waste any of the puff pastry after spending so much time and effort making it, we used the leftovers to make sweet *palmiers* and *sacristains* with sugar and cinnamon.

Nowadays I save myself the hassle and order puff pastry from my local *boulangerie*. Otherwise, you can buy pretty good puff pastry from the supermarket—make sure you get the all-butter version.

• 8 oz puff pastry

For the palmiers: 1 heaped tbsp Meaux mustard (or another grainy mustard)
• 2 handfuls of finely grated mature Comté cheese or a mature hard cheese of your choice

For the sacristains: 20 olives, pitted • 1 clove of garlic • 1 anchovy fillet

Preheat the oven to 400°F and line two baking sheets with parchment paper. Roll out the puff pastry dough between two sheets of parchment paper into a 16-by-12-inch rectangle. Cut the rectangle in half widthwise, to give two 8-by-12-inch rectangles.

TO MAKE THE *PALMIERS*: Spread the mustard over one pastry rectangle and sprinkle the cheese on top. Take one long side of the rectangle and roll it into the middle. Repeat on the other side, so that the two rolls touch each other. Wrap tightly in plastic wrap and freeze for 10 minutes* before cutting into thirty ⅜-inch-thick slices. Lay the slices on one of the prepared baking sheets.

TO MAKE THE *SACRISTAINS*: Crush the olives, garlic, and anchovy to a rough paste *(tapenade)* using a mortar and pestle or a blender. Spread the *tapenade* over the remaining pastry rectangle and then cut the rectangle into twelve 1-inch-wide strips. Take a strip and twist it, then lay it on the second baking sheet. Repeat with the remaining strips.

Bake the *palmiers* and *sacristains* for 10 minutes or until golden and crisp. Serve warm or at room temperature.

* *Both* palmiers *and* sacristains *can be frozen unbaked. Simply bake from frozen, allowing an extra couple of minutes in the oven.*

Preparation time: 30 minutes Resting time: 10 minutes
Baking time: 10 minutes

Truffes de foie gras

Foie gras truffles

One of my favorite restaurants in Paris is Le Châteaubriand, despite the fact you're at the whims of the chef, Inaki Aizpitarte, when you eat there (it's a set menu only). I've always been impressed with the way Aizpitarte combines his love of foreign cuisines with his French origins, but what I enjoy most is that the dishes are simple yet always with a special touch that makes them original.

One of the starters I have enjoyed there is foie gras sprinkled with Indian *mukhwas*, an after-dinner nibble of spice seeds and nuts that tastes sweet and refreshing. I was surprised how well they went together, and also that I actually ate it—foie gras is one of the very few foods I prefer not to eat. The whole thing got me thinking about sweet and savory combinations, and that's how this little idea came about.

• 7 oz foie gras, faux gras,* or duck liver pâté • 2 tbsp unsweetened cocoa powder
• 2 tbsp crushed gingersnaps • 2 tbsps *mukhwas* • Toast for serving

Place the foie gras in the freezer and freeze for 10 minutes until well chilled.

Cut the foie gras into fifteen–twenty 1½-inch cubes and roll into balls.** Roll some of the balls in cocoa powder, some in crushed gingersnaps, and others in *mukhwas*. Chill for at least 30 minutes or until needed. Serve in paper petit four or candy cups, with small triangles of toast.

 * *Faux gras is made from the livers of geese and ducks that have been naturally fattened rather than force-fed.*

** *If the pâté starts melting in your hands, place it back in the freezer and run your hands under cold water.*

Preparation time: 20 minutes Resting time: 10 minutes
Chilling time: 30 minutes

Les huîtres

Oysters

When to eat oysters? Well, oysters spawn in the warmer months (May to August), which makes them fatty, watery, and lacking in flavor at this time of year, whereas oysters that are harvested in the cooler, nonspawning months (the ones with the letter *r* in them) have a fresh seafood flavor and are lean with a firm texture. It's as simple as that.

Buying and storing oysters

Oysters should be tightly closed and unbroken when bought. Discard any that open. They can be kept unopened, wrapped in wet paper towels, for a couple of days in the fridge. Don't store them in an airtight container or in fresh water or they will die.

How to shuck an oyster

Use a special oyster knife (called a shucker) that has a guard and a dull blade with a pointed tip. Don't even attempt to use an ordinary knife, as you'll be more likely to stab yourself than open the oyster.

Wash and scrub the oysters under cold running water to get them clean. Using a tea towel folded double to protect your hand, place the oyster with its round bottom on a chopping board. Dig the tip of the knife into the hinge (the pointy end of the oyster) and wiggle the blade along the hinge in order to loosen it. Once the shell is loose enough, twist the knife to open the shell a little. Imagine turning a key in a car door.

Keep the knife flush with the top shell and slide it along to separate the two shells and sever the muscle in the top shell.

Lift off the top shell and remove any broken pieces of shell from the oyster flesh, being careful not to spill any of the juices.

Should the oyster smell in any way fishy or "off," discard it. Freshly shucked oysters should smell of the sea in a clean, fresh, and pleasant way.

If you want to make the oyster easier to eat, carefully detach the muscle from the bottom shell with the tip of the knife.

Les assaisonnements pour les huîtres—Condiments for oysters

An oyster purist would frown upon eating anything but the oyster, but for me a squeeze of lemon or the traditional mignonette takes the edge off the feeling of gulping down a mouthful of seawater. I also have my favorite condiments to serve with them, but go easy—you don't want to drown out the oyster's flavor.

In general when I serve oysters I reckon with at least 8 per person (the French absolutely love oysters). Each condiment recipe on page 145 is enough for 12–15 oysters (you only need about ½ teaspoon of condiment with each one as it shouldn't mask the flavor of the oyster itself). All condiments should be refrigerated for an hour before using.

Mignonette

• a pinch of sugar • a pinch of salt • 2 tbsp red wine vinegar • 1 shallot, finely diced

Dissolve the sugar and salt in the vinegar, then mix in the chopped shallot.

Calvados apple mignonette

• a pinch of sugar • a pinch of salt • 1 tbsp cider vinegar
• 1 tsp Calvados • ¼ Granny Smith apple, cored and finely diced

Dissolve the sugar and salt in the vinegar and Calvados, then mix in the apple.

Watermelon and cucumber brunoise*

• a pinch of salt • a generous pinch of sugar • 2 tbsp rice wine vinegar
• 4 tbsp finely diced watermelon flesh (without skin and seeds)
• 3 tbsp finely diced seeded cucumber

Dissolve the salt and sugar in the vinegar and pour over the watermelon and cucumber. Mix carefully together.

* Brunoise *is the French term for ingredients that have been finely diced into tiny cubes.*

Le grand aïoli avec des crudités

Garlic mayonnaise with crunchy raw vegetables

Le grand aïoli is traditionally a main course, but instead of serving the garlic mayonnaise the classic way with boiled vegetables, I serve it with raw vegetables (or *crudités* as the French call them), for extra freshness and crunch.

- a selection of seasonal raw vegetables (e.g., carrots, radishes, peppers, Belgian endive leaves, and cherry tomatoes), enough for 4 people

For the aïoli: 1 slice of white bread, crusts removed • 4 tbsp milk
• 4 cloves of garlic • 1 egg yolk • 1 cup olive oil (not extra virgin)
• 3 tbsp lemon juice • salt and pepper

Prepare the vegetables for dipping, leaving the stalks on for an attractive presentation.

TO MAKE THE *AÏOLI*: Soak the bread in the milk for 10 minutes.

Squeeze out any excess liquid from the bread, then pound the bread and garlic to a smooth paste using a mortar and pestle. Add the egg yolk and continue pounding, then start adding the olive oil a few drops at a time. Keep on pounding, slowly incorporating the remaining oil until the mayonnaise is thick, then add the lemon juice and season with salt and pepper. If not using immediately, keep in an airtight container in the fridge and use within a day. Whisk before serving, as it sometimes sets a little stiff when chilled.

Serve the *aïoli* in a bowl, surrounded by the vegetables for dipping.

Preparation time: 20 minutes

Financiers en apéritif

Aperitif financiers

According to legend, these little cakes were made by a *pâtissier* who baked in La Bourse, the financial district of Paris. He made little cakes in the shape of gold bars to sell to his financial clients, hence the name *financiers*.

Traditionally, *financiers* are sweet, but they can easily be made into a savory bite for an *apéro*, and the filling can be any ingredients you have in your fridge. Just make sure you cut them into small pieces.

• 7 tbsp butter • ½ cup ground almonds • ¼ cup all-purpose flour • 1½ tsp baking powder • ½ tsp sugar • 3 eggs, separated • ½ tsp salt • 5 oz cheese, ham, bacon, olives, cherry tomatoes, or leftover roasted vegetables (whatever you fancy really)

Preheat the oven to 350°F and butter and flour a *financier* pan.*

Start melting the butter in a pan over a medium heat. Carry on melting until the butter turns a dark golden brown (this is called *beurre noisette*), then immediately take the pan off the heat.

Mix the dry ingredients together in a bowl. Whisk the egg whites and salt to soft peaks in another bowl.

Beat the egg yolks in a third bowl, and slowly incorporate the warm butter (if the butter is still very hot, it will curdle the eggs). Sift the dry ingredients into the egg and butter mix and then fold in half the egg whites followed by the cheese, ham, bacon, etc. Fold in the rest of the egg whites.

Spoon the batter into the prepared pan and bake for 12–15 minutes or until the cakes spring back when touched. Leave to cool in the pan. *Financiers* are best eaten the same day, but will keep in an airtight container for a couple of days.

* Financier *pans usually have 20 sections, so for this recipe you will have to use the pan twice to make 30* financiers. *I have two types of pan at home—an old-fashioned metal one that needs to be buttered and floured, and a new silicone one that needs no preparation. You could use a mini tart pan instead, but you won't get the characteristic gold-bar shape that gives financiers their name.*

Preparation time: 20 minutes Baking time: 12–15 minutes

Bâtonnets de pastis

Pastis Popsicles

Pastis, the anise-flavored alcohol that is normally diluted with water (it's pretty necessary with a 40-percent alcohol content), has a bit of a reputation as a drink for pensioners who play *pétanque*. For my generation I thought I'd give pastis a little twist and a few extra ingredients. Think *mojito* meets the south of France. Frozen into Popsicles, I think it's quite a refreshing way to start an *apéro*.

• a handful of mint, leaves only • 1 lemon
• 1 tsp sugar • ⅔ cup lemonade • 3 tbsp pastis

Place a mint leaf in each of twelve mini demisphere molds.* Finely grate the lemon zest into a jug. Add the rest of the mint and the sugar to the lemon zest and mash with the end of a rolling pin or a wooden spoon. Mix in 1½ tablespoons lemon juice, the lemonade, and pastis. Pass through a sieve and pour into a jug.

Pour the liquid into the molds and freeze them for 3 hours or until solid. Remove two demispheres and place them back into one of the empty demisphere holes to form a sphere (you need to sit the demispheres upright). Insert a Popsicle stick into the gap between the two demispheres and pour in a teaspoon of cold water to help them stick together. Repeat with the other spheres to make another five Popsicles, working quickly. Refreeze for another hour or overnight, until completely frozen.

* I use a silicone mold that has fifteen demisphere holes, but if you haven't got a mold you can use an ordinary ice-cube tray to make 6–8 Popsicles (depending on the size of your tray). Pour the liquid into the compartments in the tray, then place in the freezer and leave for a couple of hours until semifrozen. Remove from the freezer and insert a Popsicle stick into the middle of each Popsicle, then return to the freezer until completely frozen.

Preparation time: 20 minutes Freezing time: 4 hours–overnight

UNE PLANCHE À DÉCOUPER

LES ALLUMETTES

LE MOULIN À POIVRE

LA POÊLE

UNE CUILLÈRE EN BOIS

LE BEURRE

UN VERRE DE VIN

LE COUTEAU

LA COCOTTE

LE RÉCHAUD À GAZ

Dinner with Friends and Family

Dîner avec les amis et la famille

LE MOULIN À POIVRE

LE TABLIER

UNE CUILLÈRE EN BOIS

LES ALLUMETTES

LE SEL

LE BOL

L'HEURE DU DÉJEUNER

LA POÊLE

LE BEURRE

L'HUILE D'OLIVE

UNE PLANCHE À DÉCOUPER

In 2010 UNESCO added French gastronomy and the ritual of the traditional French meal to its 'world's intangible heritage' list.

When I first moved to France, I didn't understand what the big fuss was about. After all, there are many other cultures that have culinary traditions that match the French. But I came to realize that it's not just about the cooking, it's about the appreciation of good food. The French understand their produce and know how it should be treated. A great example is the iconic yet humble baguette. In Paris an annual prize is awarded to the best baguette in the region. Even something as basic and affordable as bread is not taken for granted, and it's seen as not only a skill but a form of art.

The French are brought up with this understanding. It doesn't need to be taught. It's a way of life. As UNESCO acknowledged, a French meal is not only about eating. The custom of bringing people together to enjoy good food, drink and company is something the French do particularly well. It starts off with an *apéritif*, followed by four courses (starter, main course, cheese and dessert) and is finished off with a *digestif*. Dishes are carefully matched with wine. French seasonal produce, preferably local, is preferred over foreign, imported products. This is not something new. Long before 'foodtainment', celebrity chefs and the mass food media influx, i.e. the overwhelming amount of food magazines, television shows, websites, blogs, books, etc., the French were obsessed with the culinary arts.

But the French don't just discuss food and consume it, they also get a kick out of actually cooking. The art of selecting ingredients, deciding how they should be prepared and making an effort with presentation adds to the pleasure of eating. There's no better way to experience *'la joie de vivre'*, the French passion for all good things in life, than sharing a home-cooked meal with loved ones.

Galette aux pommes de terre et poires avec Roquefort

Potato and pear galette with Roquefort

A baked potato with melted cheese was one of the best lunches we had at school. You can't beat that melted cheese and potato combo. This is a slightly more sophisticated (but effortless) French homage to my humble childhood favorite.

• 4 firm-fleshed potatoes (such as fingerling) • 1 firm pear
• 3½ oz Roquefort or another blue cheese

Preheat the oven to 350°F. Peel the potatoes and cut into ⅟₁₆-inch-thick slices. On a baking sheet lined with parchment paper, overlap the potato slices tightly to make four rectangles. Peel the pear and cut into small cubes, then sprinkle the cubes over the potatoes and crumble the cheese on top. (Keep the cheese in the middle, otherwise it will drip off the potatoes when it melts.) Bake for about 20 minutes or until the potatoes turn golden brown and crisp around the edges. Serve immediately.

Preparation time: 20 minutes Baking time: 20 minutes

Asperges à la parisienne

Parisian asparagus

The Parisian part of this recipe is the sauce, which also goes by the name of *sauce allemande*. It's basically a *velouté* sauce (see page 270) enriched with egg yolks and a little cream—a great alternative to hollandaise.

For the sauce: 2 tbsp butter • ¼ cup all-purpose flour • 1¾ cups veal or beef stock, lukewarm • 2 tbsp heavy cream • 2 egg yolks • a couple of drops of lemon juice • salt and white pepper

• a pinch each of salt and sugar • 1 lb asparagus, trimmed

TO MAKE THE SAUCE: Melt the butter in a large pan over a medium heat. Add the flour and beat hard until you have a smooth paste *(roux)*. Continue beating until the *roux* begins to have a golden color. Take off the heat and gradually add the stock, whisking constantly.

Place the pan back over a medium heat and simmer gently for 10 minutes, whisking frequently. If the sauce becomes too thick, whisk in a little more stock.

Take the sauce off the heat and whisk in the cream and egg yolks. Season with lemon juice, salt, and white pepper.*

Meanwhile, bring a large pot of water to a boil. Add the salt and sugar followed by the asparagus and cook for 2 minutes or until the asparagus is tender.

Drain the asparagus well and serve immediately, with the sauce spooned over and around.

* *The sauce should be used straightaway. Do not reheat or the eggs will separate and the sauce will become lumpy.*

Preparation: 10 minutes Cooking time: 20 minutes

Endives au jambon

Belgian endive with ham

People can be put off by Belgian endive because it sometimes tastes bitter. When buying, go for the small ones that are firm and closed. These tend to be less bitter.

For the béchamel *sauce:* 2 tbsp butter • ¼ cup all-purpose flour
• 2 cups milk, lukewarm • ¼ onion, skin removed • 1 clove
• 1 bay leaf • a pinch each of white pepper and nutmeg • salt

• 4 Belgian endives • a pinch of sugar • 4 slices of ham

MAKE THE SAUCE: Melt the butter in a large pan over a medium heat. Add the flour and beat hard until you have a smooth paste. Take off the heat and leave to cool for 2 minutes, then gradually add the milk, whisking constantly. Place the pan back over a medium heat; add the onion, clove, and bay leaf, and simmer gently for 10 minutes, whisking frequently. If the sauce becomes too thick, whisk in a little more milk.

Remove the outer leaves and stems from the endives and simmer the endives in salted water with a pinch of sugar for 10–15 minutes or until tender.

Drain the endives well. Wrap a slice of ham around each one and place in individual baking dishes (or one large dish if you prefer).

Finish the sauce by removing the onion, clove, and bay leaf, then add the pepper and nutmeg and season with salt. Cover the endives with the sauce and put under a hot broiler for a couple of minutes or until golden. Serve immediately.

Preparation time: 15 minutes Cooking time: 30 minutes

Soufflé au fromage

Cheese soufflé

There are many myths about this French classic, but it mainly comes down to science—it's the heat that makes the bubbles in the egg whites expand when a soufflé is baked. There's no need to stick to the age-old rule of not daring to open the oven while the soufflé is baking. The mixture won't fall unless it actually starts to cool down and, even if it does start to sink, it will rise again. Soufflés and the stories surrounding them are, quite literally, full of hot air.

For the cheese sauce base: 3 egg yolks • 1 heaped tsp Dijon mustard
• a generous pinch each of cayenne pepper, nutmeg, and salt
• 1½ tbsp all-purpose flour • 1 cup milk
• 3½ oz Gruyère or mature Comté cheese, or a mature hard cheese of your choice, grated

• 2 tbsp soft butter, for brushing • 4–6 tbsp dried breadcrumbs*
• 4 egg whites • a pinch of salt • a couple of drops of lemon juice

TO MAKE THE CHEESE SAUCE BASE: Put the egg yolks into a bowl with the mustard, cayenne, nutmeg, and salt. Whisk until light and thick, then whisk in the flour. Bring the milk to a boil in a pan and then pour in a slow stream onto the egg mixture, whisking vigorously all the time.

Pour the mixture into a clean pan and whisk continuously over a medium heat, making sure to scrape the side and the bottom of the pan otherwise the mixture will burn. Once the sauce starts to thicken and release a bubble or two, take the pan off the heat.

Stir in the grated cheese and taste for seasoning—the sauce should be slightly overseasoned to allow for the egg whites being added later. Cover the sauce with plastic wrap, patting it down so that it sticks directly onto the sauce. Refrigerate until cool (you can prepare the sauce to this stage up to 2 days in advance).

When you are ready to make the soufflés, preheat the oven to 400°F. Brush four ramekins with softened butter, working with upward strokes from the bottom to the top. Check that the entire inside of each dish has been covered with butter before adding a heaped tablespoon of breadcrumbs. Roll and tilt each ramekin so that the breadcrumbs coat the inside evenly. »»»

In a clean glass or metal bowl, whisk the egg whites to stiff peaks with the salt and lemon juice. Beat the cold cheese sauce until smooth and then mix in half the egg whites until fully incorporated. Gently fold in the rest of the egg whites.

Divide the mix between the ramekins and tap the base of each dish on the work surface to ensure that there are no air pockets. Level the surface of each soufflé by pulling a palette knife (or the back edge of a large knife) across the top of the dish, then clean any drips off the outside or they will burn. To help the soufflés rise, run your thumbnail around the top edge of each ramekin to make a groove.

Put the ramekins into the oven immediately and reduce the temperature to 350°F. Bake for 15–20 minutes or until the soufflés have risen by two-thirds of their original size and wobble a little when moved. Serve straightaway.

* For a flavored coating, mix a generous pinch of ground cumin, chile powder, dried oregano, or finely chopped thyme or rosemary with the breadcrumbs.

Tips for a successful soufflé

• Butter (using upward brushstrokes) and coat the ramekins properly; otherwise the soufflés will stick.

• Make sure to separate the eggs carefully. Any traces of egg yolk in the whites will stop the whites whisking into peaks.

• Don't use a plastic bowl to whisk the egg whites, as traces of oil or grease from previous use may remain. Any traces of fat will stop the egg whites forming stiff peaks.

• Make sure the oven is preheated to the correct temperature. Too cold and the soufflé won't rise; too hot and it will burn on the top before being cooked through.

Preparation time: 30 minutes   Chilling time: 45 minutes
Baking time: 15–20 minutes

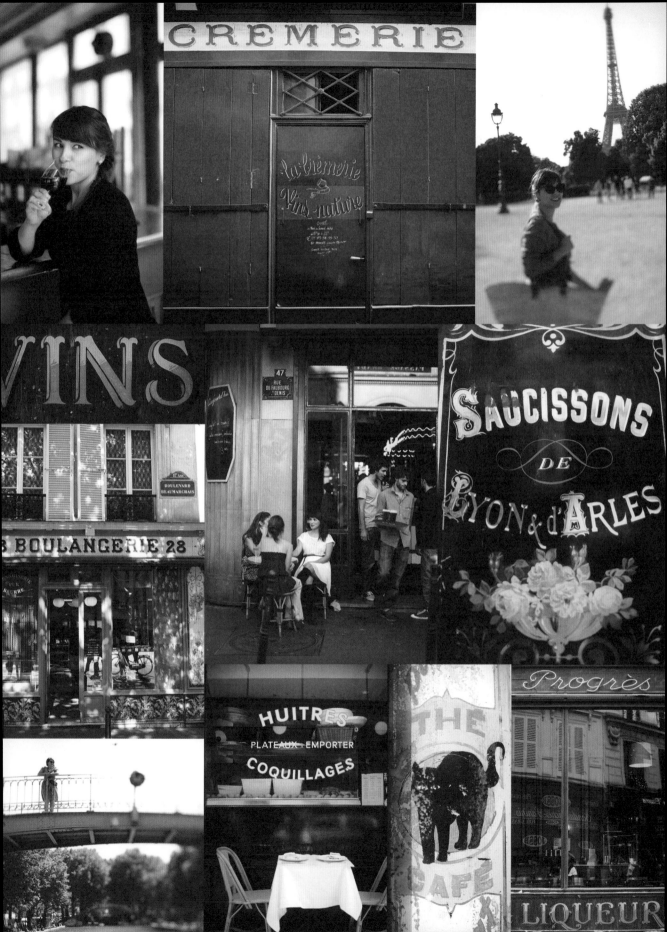

Quenelles lyonnaises au four

Baked Lyon dumplings

France's gastronomic capital is Lyon. Chef Paul Bocuse is based in the area, and two of France's favorite wines, Côtes du Rhône and Beaujolais, come from the region. Then there's the excellent produce (especially charcuterie) and the classic dish of dumplings in a creamy sauce. *Quenelles lyonnaises* are not the lead-balloon type of dumplings—whipped-up egg whites make them light and fluffy.

• 14 oz raw pike fillets,* without skin and bones • ½ cup plus 1 tbsp soft butter • 1¼ cups milk
• 1 cup plus 1½ tbsp all-purpose flour • 6 eggs, separated • 1 tsp salt
• a generous pinch each of pepper and nutmeg • a handful of chopped parsley (optional)

*For the sauce:*** 2 tbsp dry white wine • 1 tsp fish sauce • 1 tbsp tomato paste
• ⅔ cup crème fraîche • a generous pinch of cayenne pepper • a pinch of sugar

Whizz the fish and butter in a blender to make a paste. Bring the milk to a boil, add the flour, and beat hard over a low heat until it forms a ball. Leave to cool for 5 minutes, then whizz in the blender with the fish paste and egg yolks until smooth. Whisk the egg whites to soft peaks. Fold the egg whites into the fish paste and season with salt, pepper, and nutmeg. Spread the mix over a large tray and cover with plastic wrap. Refrigerate overnight.

The next day, bring a large pot of salted water to a boil and preheat the broiler on its highest setting. Using two large, deep spoons, form the mixture into *quenelle* shapes. Dip the spoons in warm water between each scoop—this will help stop the mixture sticking.

Lower the dumplings into the boiling water (in batches so as not to overcrowd the pot) and cook for 5 minutes or until they float to the surface. Use a slotted spoon to transfer them to a baking dish, being careful as they're very fragile.

TO MAKE THE SAUCE: Mix together the wine, fish sauce, tomato paste, crème fraîche, cayenne, and sugar.

Then pour the sauce over the dumplings and put under the broiler for 5–10 minutes or until golden and bubbling. If you like, sprinkle parsley on top before serving.

 * *Pike can be replaced with the fish of your choice, or even chicken breasts.*

** *The sauce can be replaced with* Sauce Béchamel *(page 269) or Escoffier's Tomato Sauce (page 271), or it can be omitted altogether and the* quenelles *simply sprinkled with grated mature cheese.*

Preparation time: 45 minutes Resting time: overnight
Cooking time: 20 minutes

Blanc-manger
aux crevettes et asperges

Shrimp and asparagus blancmange

In the Middle Ages, white chicken meat and blanched almonds were used to make *blanc-manger* (*blanc* meaning "white" and *manger* "to eat"). The delicate, sweet flavor of shrimp goes very nicely with almonds and asparagus in this cool blancmange. Perfect for a hot summer's day.

• 1 tbsp butter • 12 oz unshelled large raw shrimp • salt • 10 oz asparagus, ends trimmed
• 1⅔–2 cups unsweetened almond milk* • 1 tsp fish sauce
• a generous pinch of cayenne pepper • 4 gelatin sheets (0.07 oz per sheet)

Heat the butter in a large, deep frying pan. Add the shrimp and cook for 3 minutes or until golden brown. Leave until cool enough to handle, remove the shells and heads, and put these back in the pan. Cut the shrimp in half lengthwise and devein. Place four halved shrimp, cut-side in, against the wall of each of six disposable aluminum cups (2 inches diameter by 1½ inches deep).** Chop the rest into small cubes.

Cut the tips off the asparagus (slightly longer than the depth of the cups) and halve them length-wise. Cut the rest of the asparagus into small cubes. Blanch the asparagus tips and cubes in salted boiling water for 1 minute or until tender but slightly crunchy. Drain and hold under very cold running water for a couple of minutes. Use the tips to line the cups, squeezing them in between the shrimp.

Add 1¼ cups of the almond milk, the fish sauce, and cayenne to the shrimp shells. Cover and simmer gently for 10 minutes. Pour through a fine sieve into a pan, using the back of a spoon to press out as much liquid as possible. Measure and add more almond milk to make the total 1¼ cups. Taste for salt.

Soak the gelatin in cold water for 10 minutes or until soft. Drain and squeeze out the excess water, then dissolve in the shrimp-shell stock, whisking vigorously. (If necessary, heat very gently, stirring until the gelatin dissolves.)

Divide the shrimp and asparagus cubes between the lined cups and pour in the stock. Refrigerate for 4 hours or until set.

To serve, run a knife around the top edge of each blancmange, cut a slit on both sides of the foil, and peel away the cup.

* *You can get almond milk in some large supermarkets, health food shops, and online.*

** *Or use a muffin pan lined with paper cups and remove the blancmanges from the paper to serve.*

Preparation time: 30 minutes Cooking time: 25 minutes
Resting time: 4 hours–overnight

Sabayon aux Saint-Jacques

Scallop sabayon

Sweet sabayons are traditionally seen on dessert menus, but savory sabayons work equally well as a starter or main course. This recipe is nicely balanced, with the creaminess of the sauce, the natural sweetness of the scallops, and a kick from the peppery arugula to round everything off.

For the sabayon: 4 egg yolks • 6½ tbsp dry white wine • a pinch each of sugar and salt

• 12 large scallops • 2 tbsp olive oil • several handfuls of arugula, to garnish

TO MAKE THE SABAYON: Put the egg yolks, wine, sugar, and salt into a bain-marie (a heatproof bowl set over a pot of simmering water) and whisk until thick and foamy, about 10 minutes. To test, draw a figure eight in the mixture with the whisk—if the figure stays put, then the sabayon is ready. Take the bowl off the pan, cover with a lid or plate, and set aside in a warm place while you cook the scallops.

Rinse the scallops under cold running water and then pat dry with paper towels.

Put the olive oil into a large pan and place over a high heat. Once the oil is smoking hot, lay the scallops in the pan and reduce the heat to medium. Cook the scallops until golden on one side, about 2 minutes. Turn the scallops over, season with salt and continue to cook until the scallops are golden and slightly firm to the touch, another 2–3 minutes.

Serve the scallops immediately, with the sabayon and a garnish of arugula.

Preparation time: 10 minutes Cooking time: 20 minutes

Crème brûlée aux oignons

Onion crème brûlée

You wouldn't normally think of putting onions in a *crème brûlée*, but surprisingly the two work really well together. Slow, gentle cooking releases the natural sweetness in the onions, which marries well with the creamy base, while the cheese gives the dish a savory aspect.

• 4 large onions • 2 tbsp butter • 3½ tbsp Calvados
• 1 cup plus 2 tbsp heavy cream • ¾ cup milk • 5 egg yolks
• 2 oz Gruyère or mature Comté cheese, finely grated • salt and pepper

For the caramel topping: 2 tbsp superfine sugar • 2 tbsp raw cane sugar

Finely slice the onions. Cook the butter and onions in a large pan for 10 minutes until golden brown. Add the Calvados and cook for 10 minutes until it evaporates, stirring often to stop the onions burning. Add the cream and milk. Bring to a boil, remove from the heat, and let stand for 30 minutes.

Preheat the oven to 225°F. Pour the cream through a sieve into a pan, and press as much cream out of the onions as possible. Discard the onions. In a large bowl, lightly beat the egg yolks and stir in the cheese. Bring the cream to a boil, then pour slowly over the egg yolks and cheese, stirring constantly. Do not overbeat, as you want to avoid too many bubbles. Season. Divide the mixture between four shallow mini gratin dishes (5½ inches diameter) and place in a deep roasting pan or baking dish.

Place the pan in the oven and pour in lukewarm water to come halfway up the dishes. Bake for 30–40 minutes or until the custards are set around the edges but still slightly loose in the middle. Remove the dishes from the water and leave to cool before covering with plastic wrap (do not let the film touch the custards). Refrigerate for 4 hours or overnight (they will keep for up to 4 days).

JUST BEFORE SERVING, MAKE THE CARAMEL TOPPING: Uncover the ramekins and check to see if condensation has collected on the custards. If it has, gently place paper towels on the surface to soak up the moisture. Mix the two types of sugar together and sprinkle a nice even layer of sugar over each custard.

Stand the ramekins on a metal tray. Holding a blowtorch* 4–5 inches from the sugar and maintaining a slow and even motion, torch the sugar until just before the desired degree of doneness is reached (the sugar will cook for a few seconds after the flame has been removed).

* A blowtorch is best for caramelizing, but if you don't have one, take a large metal spoon and hold it in a gas flame until very hot (it will turn blue, almost black in color). Place the spoon on the sugar and move it around so that the heat of the spoon caramelizes the sugar.

Preparation time: 30 minutes Resting time: 4 hours–overnight
Cooking time: 1 hour

Choucroute garnie

Alsatian pork, crackling, and sausages with a "speedy" sauerkraut

A winter warmer from Alsace. Originally a one-pot stew made with fresh, cured, and smoked pork, I've broken it down into three components: a "speedy" sauerkraut with a crunch factor, a smoky bacon broth, and the meat. I'm a big fan of a crisp crackling, so I put everything in the oven rather than cook it as a stew: the flavors are the same, but the textures are different. Serve with a Dijon or grainy mustard and boiled or roasted small new potatoes.

For the bouillon: 7-oz piece of smoked bacon • 2 cups cold water

For the speedy sauerkraut: 10 juniper berries • 6½ tbsp dry white wine, ideally from Alsace • 1⅔ cups cold water • ½ cup sugar • 2 tbsp salt • 1 cup white wine vinegar • 1 lb hard white cabbage, finely shredded

• 1 lb boned pork belly with fat and skin* • salt, for sprinkling • 4 frankfurters or other smoked sausages • 4 thick slices of smoked bacon

TO MAKE THE BOUILLON: Put the smoked bacon in a pot with the water, cover, and bring to a boil. Simmer gently for 30 minutes. Drain through a very fine sieve. (This can be made in advance and kept in the fridge overnight.)

TO MAKE THE SAUERKRAUT: Put the juniper berries into a dry pan and heat. Add the wine and reduce to a couple of tablespoons, then add the water and boil. Add the sugar, salt, and vinegar and stir over a low heat until the sugar dissolves. Pour over the cabbage in a plastic container, let cool, then cover and refrigerate for 1–4 hours. (It will keep in an airtight container in the fridge for up to a week. The longer it marinates, the less crunchy it will be, but it will still be delicious.)

Preheat the oven to 500°F, or its hottest setting, and line a roasting pan with parchment paper. Pat the skin of the pork dry with paper towels** before sprinkling and rubbing with salt. Roast the pork for 10 minutes, then turn the heat down to 350°F and roast for another hour before adding the sausages and smoked bacon slices. Roast for another 30 minutes, shaking the pan and turning the sausages and bacon halfway. If the pork skin isn't crisping, turn the heat up to 425°F.

To serve, bring the bouillon to a boil and slice the crispy pork into four portions. Place the pork on individual plates with a slice of bacon, a sausage, and a spoonful of sauerkraut, then pour over a ladle of the hot bouillon.

  * *The skin must be scored. Ask your butcher, or use a very sharp knife. Don't cut through to the meat.*
** *Pourquoi? The drier the skin, the crisper the crackling.*

Preparation time: 40 minutes Cooking time: 2¼ hours

Bouillon de cassoulet avec des boulettes de canard et saucisse de Toulouse

Cassoulet soup with duck and Toulouse sausage dumplings

I first encountered *cassoulet* in jars at the supermarket, and I quickly discovered it's a dish seen more in jars than bubbling away on the kitchen stove (it's quite time-consuming to make). This recipe has the key *cassoulet* ingredients: duck, Toulouse sausage, tomato, smoked bacon, and white beans, but there's no stewing for hours. Instead of being a heavy dish, my cassoulet has a light touch, with its bouillon base, and duck and sausage dumplings.

For the dumplings: **10 oz** duck breast, fat and skin removed • **1** clove of garlic, chopped • **½** onion, chopped • **½ tsp** pepper • **10 oz** Toulouse sausages, skinned

• **10-oz** piece of smoked bacon • **⅓** cup sun-dried tomatoes, rinsed well if marinated in oil • **1 oz** dried *cèpes* or *porcini* • **7 cups** cold water • **2 tbsp** tomato paste • **1 tsp** brown sugar • **1 tsp** salt • **½ tsp** pepper • **1** cup drained canned white beans (e.g., *cannellini*, Great Northern), rinsed • **2** carrots, thinly sliced into rounds • sprigs of parsley, to garnish

TO MAKE THE DUMPLINGS: Roughly chop the duck and whizz in a blender with the garlic, onion, and pepper until the same texture as sausage meat. Using your hands, combine this mixture with the Toulouse sausage, then take about 2 tablespoons of the mixture at a time and roll into small balls. (These can be kept in an airtight container in the fridge for up to 2 days.*)

Put the bacon, sun-dried tomatoes, and dried mushrooms into a large pot with the water. Bring to a boil, cover, and simmer for 30 minutes. Take off the heat, remove the bacon, tomatoes, and mushrooms, and discard. Whisk in the tomato paste and add the sugar, salt, and pepper. Taste and adjust seasoning. (This bouillon can be kept in an airtight container in the fridge for up to 2 days.*)

Bring the bouillon to a simmer and add the beans and carrots. Simmer for 5 minutes (don't cook for too long or the beans may disintegrate). Meanwhile, heat a large nonstick frying pan until hot. Place half the dumplings in the pan and cook for 8–10 minutes, shaking the pan once in a while to stop them sticking. Remove and repeat with the remaining dumplings. Divide the dumplings among soup bowls, pour the soup over them, and garnish with parsley before serving.

* *Both the bouillon and the uncooked dumplings can be frozen for up to 2 months. Defrost the dumplings for a couple of hours before frying.*

Preparation time: 30 minutes Cooking time: about 1 hour

Bouillabaisse

Provençal fish stew

This quintessential Provençal dish from Marseille combines the best local seafood with the flavors of Provence: fennel seeds, saffron, and orange. A simple dish has evolved into something much more elaborate, and nowadays a bouillabaisse may include three types of fish and three types of shellfish. In Marseille the stock is served as a soup with *rouille* and bread, followed by the fish and vegetables. I'm going back to its roots here, omitting the large assortment of fish, keeping it simple but retaining the original flavors. By using fillets instead of whole fish, it makes the dish less daunting for guests who fear the "fish bone in throat" situation. Hand the *rouille* round in a bowl, with crusty bread.

For the rouille: 2 cloves of garlic • 1 egg yolk
• a pinch each of cayenne pepper and saffron threads • 1 cup sunflower oil • salt

For the soup base: 4 tbsp olive oil • 1 onion, finely chopped • 4 cloves of garlic, crushed to a paste
• 2 tbsp tomato paste • 2 star anise • 1 tsp fennel seeds • 1 bay leaf • 3 sprigs of thyme
• zest of 1 orange • a pinch of chile powder • 1 tsp saffron threads
• 1 stick of celery, finely sliced • 1 bulb of fennel, finely sliced • 3 large tomatoes, roughly chopped
• ⅔ cup dry white wine • 4½ cups fish stock • juice of 1 orange (3½ tbsp)

• 14 oz fish fillets of your choice (I use hake, pollack, and salmon), cut into large chunks
• 1 lb mussels, cleaned • 1 lb shrimp, no shells • salt and pepper
• a couple of green onions, finely sliced

TO MAKE THE *ROUILLE*: Crush the garlic cloves to a fine paste in a large bowl. Add the egg yolk, cayenne, and saffron. Drizzle the oil slowly into the bowl, whisking hard (you can use an electric whisk). Taste for salt, cover, and refrigerate until you are ready to serve.*

TO MAKE THE SOUP BASE: Heat the olive oil in a large pot and add the onion, garlic, tomato paste, star anise, fennel seeds, bay leaf, thyme, orange zest, chile powder, saffron, celery, fennel, and tomatoes. Cook until the onion is soft, then add the wine and reduce by half. Pour in the stock and orange juice, bring to a rapid boil, and cook for 10 minutes.

Lower the heat and add the seafood, then cover and simmer gently for 5 minutes, shaking the pan a few times. Taste for seasoning before serving sprinkled with the green onions.

* *The* rouille *is best made on the day of serving, because of the raw egg yolk, but you can make the soup base the day before as this will give the flavors time to develop. When ready to serve, simply bring to a boil and throw in the seafood.*

Preparation time: 30 minutes Cooking time: 25 minutes

Poisson meunière

Fish with lemon and brown butter sauce

Meunière translates as "miller's wife," referring to the flour used to dredge the fish before it is cooked. This acts as a protective barrier, preventing the delicate flesh from drying out. I use lemon sole for my *meunière* (Dover sole is just too expensive), but why not try other fish such as Pacific halibut or even trout? If you have a reputable local fishmonger, have a chat with him to see what he recommends. A key factor in making this dish delicious is the brown butter and lemon sauce, although the capers and chopped parsley make a tasty addition too.

• 2 fillets of lemon sole (about 5 oz each), skin removed
• 3 tbsp all-purpose flour • ½ tsp salt • a generous pinch of pepper
• 1½ tbsp sunflower oil • 3 tbsp butter, cut into cubes • juice of ½ lemon
• 1 tbsp chopped parsley • 1 tbsp small capers (optional)

Check the fish for small bones and use tweezers to pull out any that you find.

Mix the flour with the salt and pepper and spread out over a large plate. Pat the fish fillets in the flour so they are evenly coated, and shake off any excess.

Heat the oil in a large frying pan over a high heat, When the oil is smoking hot, place the fish fillets, fleshy-side down, in the pan and lower the heat to medium. Cook for 1–2 minutes on one side until golden, then turn the fillets over and cook for another 1–2 minutes until the second side is golden.* Place the fish on a warmed plate and cover with aluminum foil.

Wipe the pan with paper towels and return to a medium heat. Add the cubes of butter and heat until they melt and become light brown, then turn off the heat and add the lemon juice (stand back a little as it will splatter). Add the parsley and capers (if using) and swirl the contents of the pan around. Return the fish to the pan, spoon over the juices, and serve immediately.

* Flat fish fillets need only 1–2 minutes cooking on each side. If you're cooking thicker slices or fillets from a fish like trout (¾–1¼ inches thick), then 3–4 minutes on each side should be fine.

Preparation time: 10 minutes   Cooking time: 10 minutes

Brochettes au coq au vin

Coq au vin on skewers

Rooster stewed in red wine for several hours is traditional *coq au vin*. I thought I'd shake that on its head and make a barbecue version with a red wine dipping sauce.

For the marinade: 2 cloves of garlic, finely chopped • 1 onion, finely chopped
• 2 tbsp butter • 4 small sprigs of thyme • 3 bay leaves • 2 cups red wine

• 1½ lb boned chicken legs, with skin on* • 5 oz lardons or cubes of smoked bacon
• 2 large carrots, cut into large chunks • 8 small new potatoes
• 8 small button onions, peeled and left whole • 1 tbsp red wine vinegar
• 1 tbsp cornstarch • 1 tbsp sugar • salt and pepper
• 8 small button mushrooms, brushed or peeled • 1 tbsp olive oil

8 barbecue skewers—if they're bamboo, soak them in water for at least an hour before using

TO MAKE THE MARINADE: Fry the garlic and onion in the butter until golden brown. Add the thyme and bay leaves and cook for another minute before adding the wine. Bring to a boil and simmer for 10 minutes. Leave to cool.

Cut the chicken into large chunks, place in a large plastic container with the lardons, and add the cold marinade. Cover and marinate in the fridge for at least 4 hours (best overnight).

Lift the chicken and lardons out of the marinade, then strain through a sieve. Measure 1¼ cups marinade, pour it into a pan, and set aside. Put the carrots, potatoes, and onions into a large pan of cold salted water and bring to a boil. Parboil for 5 minutes, then drain the vegetables into a sieve and hold under cold running water for 2 minutes. Leave to cool.

On a high heat, reduce the marinade by half before adding the vinegar. Mix the cornstarch to a thin paste with some water, whisk into the sauce, and boil for 5 minutes or until the consistency of heavy cream. Add the sugar and season with salt and pepper. Cover with plastic wrap, pressing it down in direct contact with the sauce. Keep the sauce warm until needed.

Thread the chicken onto the skewers, alternating with the lardons, parboiled vegetables, and mushrooms. Brush with the olive oil before cooking on the barbecue (or indoors on a griddle pan) for around 5 minutes, turning regularly. To check the chicken is cooked, cut a piece open—the juices should run clear, not red or pink. Serve with the sauce (reheated in a pan or microwave if necessary).

* *Chicken legs have more flavor and tend to be juicier than breast, or you could use boneless chicken thighs (skin on) instead. Breast meat will be fine too, as long as you are careful not to overcook it.*

Preparation time: 1 hour Resting time: 4 hours–overnight
Cooking time: 20 minutes

Poulet au citron et lavande

Lemon and lavender chicken

The lavender fields in Provence are a spectacular sight, but if you can't make it to see them, I think that using a little lavender in your cooking is probably the next best thing. In moderation, lavender tastes delicious in both savory and sweet dishes, but don't use too much or they'll start tasting like granny's soap. A crisp green salad and some boiled new potatoes are a great match for this summery dish.

For the marinade: 2 tbsp dried lavender • 4 tbsp olive oil
• 4 tbsp lavender honey or plain runny honey • 2 sprigs of thyme
• finely grated zest and juice of 1 lemon

• 1 chicken, cut into 8–10 pieces • a generous pinch of salt

TO MAKE THE MARINADE: Crush the lavender using either a mortar and pestle or a rolling pin. Put the crushed lavender into a large bowl with the oil, honey, thyme, lemon zest, and juice. Mix well.

Place the chicken pieces in a large plastic container. Pour the marinade over the chicken and make sure all the pieces are well coated. Cover and leave to marinate for 30 minutes (or up to 4 hours).

When you are ready to cook, preheat the oven to 400°F. Put the chicken and marinade into a roasting pan and sprinkle with the salt. Roast the chicken for 45 minutes, turning the pieces over halfway. To check if the chicken is done, pierce the thickest part of the flesh with a skewer—the juices should run clear, not red or pink.

Serve the chicken with the cooking juices poured over and around.

Preparation time: 10 minutes Resting time: 30 minutes–4 hours
Cooking time: 45 minutes

Poulet aux champignons avec une sauce au vin blanc

Chicken and mushrooms in a white wine sauce

You can't go wrong with this classic, and the white wine sauce is great to know. You can flavor it with fresh herbs, such as parsley, tarragon, or dill, and use it with many other ingredients besides chicken and mushrooms. I like it with poached fish or vegetables (especially leeks and boiled potatoes), and it's also an easy way to make something tasty out of leftovers—it's really good poured over roast chicken or turkey. Serve with steamed rice or pasta.

For the sauce: 2 tbsp butter • ¼ cup all-purpose flour • 2 cups chicken stock, lukewarm
• ½ cup dry white wine • 4 tbsp heavy cream • 1 tsp lemon juice • salt and pepper

• 2 tbsp butter • 1 lb chicken or turkey breast, cut into chunks
• 8 oz button mushrooms, brushed or peeled, then sliced
• a handful of finely chopped tarragon or parsley

TO MAKE THE SAUCE: Melt the butter in a large pan over a medium heat. Add the flour and beat hard until you have a smooth paste *(roux)*. Continue to beat until the *roux* begins to have a golden color. Take off the heat and gradually add the stock, whisking constantly.

Place the pan back over a medium heat and simmer gently for 10 minutes, whisking frequently to ensure none of the sauce burns on the bottom of the pan. If the sauce becomes too thick, whisk in a little more stock.

Add the wine and continue simmering for 10 minutes, then take off the heat and whisk in the cream and lemon juice. Taste for salt and pepper.

While the sauce is simmering, melt the butter in a large frying pan until sizzling, add the chicken, and fry for a few minutes until golden. Add the mushrooms and fry for another 5 minutes or until the chicken is cooked through.

To serve, mix the sauce with the chicken and mushrooms and sprinkle with some fresh tarragon.

Preparation time: 15 minutes Cooking time: 30 minutes

Blanquette de veau

Veal ragout

The French like their one-pot wonders—*coq au vin, boeuf bourguignon,* and *pot-au-feu,* for instance. *Blanquette de veau* is another "throw it all in the pot" type of dish, and it's actually simpler than many other stews, as there's no browning of the meat to be done—hence the name *blanquette.*

Normally some of the stock is combined with egg yolks and cream to make a rich white sauce, but as this dish should be about keeping work to a minimum, why bother when you can make a pretty mean sauce with just a tub of crème frâiche (full fat, please), some orange zest, and black pepper? My *caviste* (wine guy) gave me the tip of adding orange zest to the stew. Boiled potatoes, rice, or even pasta go nicely with this dish.

• 2-lb piece of veal belly (breast) with skin • 10 button onions, peeled
• 6 carrots, cut into chunks • 1 bay leaf • 1 sprig of rosemary • 1 sprig of thyme
• 10 peppercorns • a bunch of parsley stalks
• pared zest of 2 oranges • 10 button mushrooms, brushed or peeled • salt

For the sauce: 7 tbsp crème fraîche • finely grated zest of 1 orange • salt and pepper

Preheat the oven to 325°F. Place the meat in a large ovenproof pot with all the other ingredients except the mushrooms and salt. Pour in cold water until the meat and vegetables are submerged, then cover the pot with its lid, place in the oven, and cook for 2 hours.

Take the pot out of the oven. Remove the meat, onions, and carrots from the stock and set aside. Tip the contents of the pot into a very fine sieve or coffee filter set over a bowl and let the stock run through (to remove any impurities).

Pour the stock into a clean pot and add the meat, onions, carrots, and mushrooms. Simmer gently for about 5 minutes or until the mushrooms are cooked. Taste for salt.

TO MAKE THE SAUCE: Mix the crème fraîche with the orange zest and season with salt and pepper.

Lift the meat out of the stock and cut into slices. Serve each person with a slice of veal, a spoonful of vegetables, a ladleful of stock, and a large helping of the sauce.

Preparation time: 20 minutes Cooking time: 2–2½ hours

Bœuf bourguignon avec des quenelles de baguettes

Burgundy beef with baguette dumplings

Each region in France uses their own local red wine for this dish, so you don't need to use a bottle of Burgundy. The idea of the dumplings came to me when I started accumulating odd ends of leftover baguettes. They make a great alternative to potatoes, as well as soaking up the juices from the stew.

- 2 lb beef shin or stewing beef, cut into 6 large chunks • 3–4 tbsp all-purpose flour
- 2 tbsp vegetable oil • 5 oz lardons or cubes of smoked bacon
- 10 button onions or shallots, peeled • 2 cloves of garlic, crushed until flat • 1 bay leaf
- a bunch of parsley stalks • 1 sprig of thyme • 1 sprig of rosemary • 3 cloves
- 10 peppercorns, crushed • 2 cups red wine • 1¼ cups water • 1 tbsp tomato paste
- a pinch of sugar • 7 oz stale baguette or other bread (crust included) • 1 cup milk
- a pinch of nutmeg • salt and pepper • a handful of chopped parsley • 1 egg
- 10 chestnut mushrooms • 2 tbsp butter, for frying

Preheat the oven to 300°F. Dust the meat with 2 tablespoons of the flour. Heat the oil in a large casserole dish over a high heat and fry the meat in batches until browned. Remove each batch, then fry the lardons, onions, garlic, herbs, and spices in the same pan until golden brown. Return the meat to the pan and add the wine, water, tomato paste, and sugar. Scrape up the caramelized bits—they will add flavor. Cover, place in the oven, and cook for 3 hours or until the meat is tender and almost falling apart.*

Cut the baguette into small cubes and place in a bowl. Bring the milk to a boil and pour over. Stir so that the milk is absorbed evenly, then cover and leave for 15 minutes. Season with nutmeg, salt, and pepper; stir in two-thirds of the chopped parsley and the egg; and mix in 1 tablespoon flour. If the mix is too wet (it should be moist and only slightly sticky), add the remaining tablespoon of flour. Wet your hands a little to help stop the dough sticking to them, then make 12–14 dumplings (smaller than a golf ball).*

About 20 minutes before the stew is ready, add the mushrooms and season with salt. Heat the butter in a large frying pan and fry the dumplings on a medium heat for 5 minutes or until golden brown and crisp, then drain. Garnish the stew with parsley and serve with the dumplings.

* *Make the stew the day before to give the flavors time to develop. Add the mushrooms before gently reheating (no boiling). The dumplings can be kept in an airtight container in the fridge for 2 hours.*

Preparation time: 45 minutes Cooking time: 3 hours

"One of the best things about Paris is being able to shop at small independent grocery shops that are still affordable. I'm lucky to have a great family-run butcher in my neighborhood. They have a brilliant selection of meat and are always happy to give you some advice on how to cook it."

Mini chevreuil en croûte

Mini Venison Wellington

I've made countless *boeufs en croûte* with the traditional mushroom filling and puff pastry, but I've found the recipe is equally good with venison, red onions, and Armagnac, whose caramel notes work particularly well with the natural sweetness in the onions.

- 4 venison (or beef) steaks, each about 6 oz and ¾ inch thick • salt and pepper
- 3 large red onions, finely sliced • 4 tbsp butter • a pinch of sugar
- a generous pinch of salt • 2 tbsp Armagnac
- 1 lb puff pastry or croissant dough,* cut into quarters • 3 tbsp Dijon mustard
- 1 egg mixed with 2 tbsp water, for the egg wash

Place a large nonstick frying pan over the highest possible heat. Season the meat all over with salt and pepper. When the pan is smoking hot, put in the steaks and sear for 30 seconds on each side. Remove and set aside for later. In the same pan over a medium heat, gently cook the onions with the butter, sugar, and salt for 20 minutes until caramelized and soft. Add the Armagnac and cook, stirring occasionally, for 10 minutes until the onions become drier. Leave to cool for 10 minutes before blending to a smooth paste. Refrigerate for about an hour until cold (or freeze for speed).

Between two sheets of parchment paper, roll out one-quarter of the pastry to a ¼-inch-thick rectangle. Cut in half widthwise to make two squares slightly larger than the steaks. Repeat with the remaining pastry to make eight squares. Preheat the oven to 400°F and line a baking sheet with parchment paper.

Brush some mustard all over a piece of steak, then place the steak in the middle of a square of pastry. Top the steak with a heaped tablespoon of the onion mix, brush egg wash around the pastry edges, and cover with another pastry square. Press the edges to seal, then trim the excess pastry to leave a ⅜-inch border and crimp with a fork. Repeat with the other pieces of pastry and the remaining 3 steaks. Cut a little cross in the top of each parcel and brush the pastry with egg wash. Place the parcels on the prepared sheet and bake for 12 minutes for medium-rare meat.** Remove from the oven, cover with aluminum foil, and leave to rest for 5 minutes before serving.

* I order puff pastry and croissant dough from the bakery if I haven't time to make it, or even buy it at the supermarket, picking one made with all butter (no palm oil, emulsifers, additives, etc.).

** If you have a meat thermometer, push it into the cross in the top of one of the parcels to check the internal temperature of the meat. 130–138°F medium-rare (red in the center), 140–151°F medium (pink in the center), 153–160°F well-done (gray-brown throughout).

Preparation time: 30 minutes Resting time: 1 hour
Cooking time: 45 minutes

Pot-au-feu de joue de boeuf

Beef cheek "pot-on-the-fire"

Almost every cuisine has a famous one-pot dish that benefits from sitting on the stove for several hours. The French are pretty clever with their pot-au-feu, making a simple one pot work as two courses. The broth makes a dark and delicious consommé starter, then the meat and vegetables are served as a main course with the traditional condiments of mustard, cornichons, and salt, plus bowls of Spicy Green Sauce and Cream Sauce (page 200).

Pop the pot on the stove mid-morning and it'll be perfect for dinner. It's actually even better made a day in advance and gently warmed up just before serving. Who said you had to slave away in the kitchen to be a French domestic goddess?

- 2–3 beef cheeks* (total weight 3 lb), fat removed and each cheek cut in half
- 2 lb oxtail or veal knuckles, chopped • 1 bouquet garni (2 bay leaves, 2 sprigs of thyme, 6 sprigs of parsley, 10 peppercorns, 5 cloves) • 2 onions, quartered with skin left on
- 2 sticks of celery • 6 carrots, 4 quartered • 4 turnips, 1 halved, 3 quartered
- 10 button onions, peeled and left whole (or 2 regular onions, quartered)
- salt and pepper • 1 bay leaf, to garnish

Put the meat and bones into a large pot, cover with cold water, and bring slowly to a simmer. Drain and discard the water, then rinse the bones, meat, and pot with cold water to remove the impurities.

Place the bones and meat back in the clean pot, cover with cold water again, and bring slowly to a "barely there" simmer. Skim off any foam that comes to the surface and then add the bouquet garni, quartered onions, celery, 2 carrots, and the halved turnip. Continue to simmer very gently (around 175°F), uncovered, until the meat is tender and almost falling apart. This can take 6–8 hours. Make sure the meat is always submerged, topping up with cold water if necessary.

Once the meat is cooked, remove it from the broth and pour the contents of the pan into a fine sieve or coffee filter set over a bowl. Discard the vegetables and anything else that doesn't filter through.

To finish, pour the broth into a clean pot and add the meat and fresh vegetables (the quartered carrots and turnips and button onions). Simmer for 30 minutes or until the vegetables are cooked. Taste for seasoning and garnish with a bay leaf.

At the table, spoon the meat and vegetables into bowls with a little of the broth and hand round any condiments. »»»

To serve the *pot-au-feu* the next day:

After cooking and separating the broth and meat, refrigerate them in separate airtight containers overnight. The next day, the broth will have set as a jelly with the impurities settled as a dark layer at the bottom. Put the top, clear part of the jelly into a pot with the meat and fresh vegetables and heat gently until the jelly has melted. Top up with a little water if needed to cover everything and simmer gently for 30 minutes or until the vegetables are cooked. Taste for seasoning. This technique will make a clearer broth.

* *If you want to use the traditional cuts of beef, such as rib, shoulder, or leg, ask the butcher to tie the meat with a string (to stop it from falling apart). Poultry, game, or lamb on the bone can be used instead of the beef cheeks and oxtail. Cooking time will vary depending on the size and type of meat; e.g., a whole chicken, cut into 8–10 pieces, will take 1½ hours (plus 30 minutes for the fresh vegetables). Lamb shanks will take 3–4 hours, depending on their size (plus 30 minutes for the fresh vegetables).*

Preparation time: 30 minutes Cooking time: 6½–8½ hours

Spicy green sauce

• ½ long red chile, seeded • 1 clove of garlic • ½ bunch of curly parsley (stalks included) • 5 tbsp red wine vinegar • 5 tbsp olive oil • 1 tsp sugar • salt (optional)

Blend all the ingredients together (except salt) until you have a thick paste. Taste and season with salt, if necessary. Refrigerate until needed (can be kept in an airtight container in the fridge for several days).

Cream sauce

• 1 cup crème fraîche • 10 cornichons, finely chopped • 1 tsp Dijon mustard • 1 tsp sugar • 2 tbsp lemon juice • salt (optional)

Mix all the ingredients together (except salt). Taste and season with salt, if necessary. Refrigerate until needed (can be kept in an airtight container in the fridge for several days).

Fajitas de pot-au-feu

French beef stew fajitas

Fajitas de pot-au-feu may not sound like a French recipe, but in essence it is—*pot-au-feu* leftovers are wrapped in tortillas with the addition of some crunchy vegetables. I make my own tortillas, but you can buy them ready-made at the supermarket.

For the tortillas: 1⅔ cups all-purpose flour • 1 tsp baking powder
• 1 tsp salt • ¾ cup plus 1 tbsp milk, lukewarm • 2 tbsp vegetable oil

• 3 tbsp olive oil • 7 oz leftover meat from *Pot-au-feu* (page 199) or leftover roast meat, shredded with a fork • 2 carrots, shaved into thin strips or grated • ¼ red cabbage, shredded

To serve: Cream Sauce and Spicy Green Sauce (page 200)

TO MAKE THE TORTILLAS: Mix the flour, baking powder, and salt together in a bowl. Add the milk and oil and use your fingertips to mix the ingredients together. Once the dough has formed a sticky ball, turn it out onto a floured surface and knead for 5 minutes. It will become less sticky the more you knead it, so don't use too much flour at the beginning. Grease a bowl with some oil before placing the dough into it and covering. Leave to rest for 20 minutes.

Put a large nonstick frying pan over a medium to high heat. Divide the dough into six small balls, and dust your work surface and rolling pin with a little flour. Roll out a ball of dough into a small, thin disk (roughly 6 inches in diameter and ¹⁄₁₆ inch thick).

Place the tortilla in the pan and cook for about a minute until golden on each side. Repeat the process to make 6 tortillas in total, then wrap the tortillas in aluminum foil and keep them warm in the oven until you are ready to serve.

Put 1 tablespoon of the olive oil into a large pan and set on a medium heat. Add the shredded meat and cook for several minutes until hot and slightly caramelized. Meanwhile, put the carrots and cabbage in a bowl and toss togther with the remaining 2 tablespoons olive oil.

TO SERVE: Spread 1 teaspoon of cream sauce over each tortilla. Add some meat and vegetables, and top with green sauce. Alternatively, set bowls of each ingredient and the tortillas on the table for everyone to help themselves.

Preparation time: 20 minutes
Resting time: 20 minutes Cooking time: 15 minutes

Steak et frites de légumes racines

Steak and root-vegetable fries

Juicy steak with crisp fries—a match made in heaven. There are different cuts—*entrecôte* (rib eye), *filet* (fillet), *bavette* (skirt), *rumsteack* (rump), *faux-filet* (sirloin)—but the method stays the same (first sear and then finish in the oven) unless the meat is less than ⅜ inch thick or is to be served rare. So there's not much to it, apart from letting the steak rest after cooking—this will make a world of difference.

For the fries: 3½ tbsp ground almonds • 2 tbsp sunflower oil • salt and pepper
• 1 sweet potato, cut into thin strips • 1 parsnip, cut into thin strips
• 1 large carrot, cut into thin strips

• 1 rib-eye steak (about 1 lb) • salt and pepper • *Sauce tartare* (page 273), optional

TO MAKE THE FRIES: Preheat the oven to 400°F. In a large bowl, mix together the ground almonds, oil, ½ teaspoon salt, and some pepper. Toss the vegetables in the mix and then spread them out in a single layer over a baking sheet. Bake for 30 minutes or until crisp, shaking the sheet halfway through.

Season the steak with salt and pepper on both sides. Heat a nonstick frying pan on a high heat. When it is so hot you can't hold your hand over it, sear the steak in the pan for 2 minutes on each side. Depending how you want it done,* put the steak in the oven with the fries for 5–10 minutes. Once the steak is cooked, wrap in foil and leave to rest on a warm plate for 10 minutes.

Unwrap the steak and cut in half. Serve straightaway with the fries, and with *Sauce tartare*.

* *There are roughly four degrees of "doneness." To test whether it is done to your liking, press your finger on the steak and gauge how it feels (see below), or you can use a meat thermometer.*

Rare—*bleu: pinch your thumb and index finger together. Feel the fleshy part of your palm below the thumb and this should have the firmness of a rare steak. Sear only—there is no need to finish cooking in the oven. Color: very red. Meat temperature: 125–130°F.*

Medium-rare—*à point: as for rare, but with your thumb and middle finger together. Sear, then finish cooking in the oven. Color: red in the center. Meat temperature 130–140°F.*

Medium—*cuit: as for rare, but with your ring finger and thumb together. Sear, then finish cooking in the oven. Color: pink in the center. Meat temperature 140–151°F.*

Well-done—*bien cuit: as for rare, but with your little finger and thumb together. Sear, then finish cooking in the oven. Color: gray-brown throughout. Meat temperature 153–160°F.*

Preparation time: 20 minutes Cooking time: 30 minutes

Canard à l'Orangina

Duck with fizzy orange

When I was invited to a dinner hosted by Chef Jean-François Piège, he described how his previous elaborate style of cooking at the Hôtel de Crillon had evolved into something a lot more simple and homely at his current restaurant in the Hôtel Thoumieux. He told an amusing story of how his wife wanted *duck à l'orange* for Sunday supper and all he could find at his local corner shop was Orangina, so he used it to make a sauce for the duck. I'm not sure exactly how he made his *canard à l'Orangina*, but here's my version. A simple watercress or wild arugula salad works well with this dish.

For the marinade: finely grated zest and juice of 1 orange • 1 tbsp olive oil
• ½ tsp ground cumin • 1 tsp salt

• 4 duck legs • 7 tbsp orange soda • 2 tbsp Cointreau
• a pinch of salt • 1 tsp red wine vinegar • 4 oranges, cut into segments

TO MAKE THE MARINADE: Mix together the orange zest and juice with the olive oil, cumin, and salt.

Rub the marinade over the duck legs and leave to marinate for a minimum of an hour (or in the fridge overnight).

Preheat the oven to 325°F. Put the duck legs with the marinade into a roasting pan and cook for 1 hour or until tender. Halfway through cooking, baste the duck with some of the pan juices.

Fifteen minutes before serving, pour the orange soda and Cointreau into a large frying pan, place on a high heat, and simmer until reduced by half. Stir in the salt and vinegar before adding the orange segments. Simmer for another 5 minutes.

Serve the duck legs hot, with the orange segments and sauce.

Preparation time: 20 minutes Resting time: 1 hour–overnight
Cooking time: 1 hour

Magret de canard avec salade d'endives et framboises

Duck breast with an endive and raspberry salad

There's a bit of a color theme going on with this dish—red raspberries and endives with pink from the duck—but that's not the reason why I put these ingredients together. The tartness of the raspberries and the bitterness of the endives are divine with the gamey taste of the duck. Serve with some crusty bread to mop up the juices, or with diced boiled potatoes that have been panfried in some of the duck fat.

• 2 large duck breasts (magrets), skin on • salt and pepper
• 4 small red Belgian endives or radicchio
• ½ cup extra virgin olive oil • 4 tbsp raspberry vinegar
• 1-pt basket of raspberries

Trim some of the fat off the duck breasts and score the skin. Rub salt and pepper on both sides of the breasts.

Place a large frying pan over a high heat. When the pan is so hot that you can't hold your hand over it, place the duck breasts, skin-side down, in the pan and turn the heat down to medium-high. Fry the breasts for 4–5 minutes on each side or until golden brown and cooked to your liking (see *Steak et frites*, page 205). You may want to drain off some of the fat while cooking, but don't throw it away—duck fat is excellent for roasting potatoes. Once the duck is cooked to your liking, remove the breasts from the pan, wrap them in aluminum foil, and leave to rest on a warm plate for 10 minutes.

Meanwhile, wash and dry the salad leaves. If they are big, cut them into smaller pieces. Put the leaves into a large bowl and sprinkle with the olive oil, vinegar, and seasoning to taste. Toss well, then scatter over four plates with the raspberries.

Carve the duck into very thin slices and divide between the plates to serve.

Preparation time: 20 minutes   Resting time: 10 minutes
Cooking time: 8–10 minutes

Sweet Treats

Gourmandises

LES AMANDES · LE SUCRE · LA FRAISE · LA GOUSSE DE VANILLE · L'ORANGE · LA MARYSE

LA FARINE · LE LAIT · LE ROMARIN · LE CAFÉ · LE BLANC D'ŒUF LE JAUNE D'ŒUF · LES CERISES

LE ROULEAU À PÂTISSERIE · LA POIRE

LA CRÈME CHANTILLY · LA FARINE

LE FOUET · LE ROULEAU À PÂTISSERIE · LA GOUSSE DE VANILLE · LE ROMARIN · LE SUCRE · LA RHUBARBE

LES AMANDES · L'ORANGE · LA MARYSE · LA FRAISE · LES TOMATES CERISE · LE THÉ

I've met quite a few foreigners who moved to Paris because they fell madly in love with a Frenchie. But it wasn't a charming Frenchman sweeping me off my feet that made me pack my bags and cross the channel.

While window-shopping on a school trip to Paris, I fell under the spell of French cakes in all sorts of shapes and sizes. Sugar-coated, they glistened in the windows of the *pâtisseries* with the sweet promise of delighting my taste buds. I was quite literally licking the windows, as in the French idiom for window-shopping: *faire du lèche-vitrine*.

Not content with eating them, I wanted to know the secrets of making them. So I enrolled in a *pâtisserie* course at Le Cordon Bleu, Paris. Before I was even let anywhere close to the kitchen, I was drilled to say *"Oui, chef."* Several hundred eggs and tons of sugar, flour, and butter later, I had learned how to whip up some of the sweet culinary delights I had seen in the *pâtisserie* windows.

One thing I learned quickly was that these recipes have to be followed to a T, unlike cooking, where you can follow your own taste. *Pâtisserie* is a science. Too much of a certain ingredient can cause total chaos with the end result. The ingredients used in French *pâtisserie* aren't that many: butter, sugar, eggs, and flour usually suffice to create something that will tantalize everyone's taste buds.

French *pâtisserie* is founded on key recipes and techniques. Certain recipes like *crème pâtissière* or short-crust pastry are considered building blocks. Once you've mastered a few, you can easily adapt them to make a broad range of other desserts.

This chapter covers a wide array of French desserts: some are simple and others a little more complicated. The more complex desserts are broken down into several shorter recipes (which in some cases can be used on their own). Don't be put off by the length. Take your time to read through the recipe, set up your equipment, and measure your ingredients before you start making the dessert—just a few tips I learned at culinary school. With a little practice, you'll be able to use some of the key recipes to make your own French-inspired creations.

Café Gourmand

This has to be one of the best ideas to appear on bistro and restaurant menus. I've always had a hard time making up my mind what to order for dessert, but with *Café Gourmand* you get three mini versions instead of having to choose just one. It's the perfect solution for my indecisive self.

To make all three mini desserts you will need one quantity of *Crème Pâtissière* recipe, which you should make in advance and chill in the fridge. The mousse and trifles can be made the day before serving, but the tartlets are best done not too far in advance or the shortbread will go a little soft.

Orange mousse

- 1 tbsp Cointreau or other orange-flavored liqueur
- 4 heaped tbsp orange marmalade • finely grated zest of 1 orange
- 1 cup chilled *Crème Pâtissière* (page 274)
- ⅔ cup heavy cream, whipped

Mix the liqueur with the marmalade and divide between four glasses. Save a little of the orange zest for the decoration; add the rest to the pastry cream and beat until smooth. Fold in half the whipped cream to lighten the mixture and then fold in the rest. Divide the mousse between the glasses, then tap each glass on the work surface to make sure that there are no air pockets. Chill for at least an hour before serving. »»

Black currant trifles

• 4 ladyfingers • 4 tbsp crème de cassis
• 1 cup chilled *Crème Pâtissière* (page 274)
• ½ cup black currants, stalks removed, plus 4 small sprigs for decoration
• sugar (optional) • 7 tbsp heavy cream, whipped

Break a ladyfinger into small pieces and fit them into the bottom of a glass. Repeat with three more glasses. Pour 1 tablespoon crème de cassis into each glass. Beat the pastry cream until smooth. Crush the black currants a little and mix with the pastry cream. If the black currants are very sour, add a little sugar. Divide the pastry cream between the glasses, then tap each glass on the work surface to make sure that there are no air bubbles. Top with whipped cream. Chill for at least an hour before serving decorated with sprigs of black currants.

Strawberry tartlets

• 1 cup chilled *Crème Pâtissière* (page 274)
• 4 round shortbread biscuits • 12–15 strawberries

Beat the pastry cream until smooth. Put it into a piping bag fitted with a round ⅜-inch nozzle and pipe a small blob in the middle of each biscuit (leave some room around the edge for the strawberries). Cut the strawberries in half and stick them around the pastry cream. Serve as soon as you can.

Preparation time: 45 minutes
Resting time: 1 hour (for the pastry cream)
Cooking time: 20 minutes

SERVES 4

Les soufflés

Soufflés

Soufflés have a reputation for being difficult, but they really aren't as daunting as you think. A sweet soufflé is simply a meringue mixture folded into pastry cream and baked.

The great thing about this recipe is that you can prepare half of it in advance, leaving you with just some last-minute whisking and folding while the oven is preheating. Pop the soufflés in the oven and 20 minutes later you can impress your guests with a magnificently risen dessert.

• 4 tbsp soft butter • 6 tbsp raw cane sugar*

For the meringue: 2 egg whites • ½ cup confectioners' sugar
• a couple of drops of lemon juice • a pinch of salt

• 1½ cups chilled *Crème Pâtissière* (page 274), with flavoring of your choice

Preheat the oven to 400°F. Brush four ramekins with soft butter, working with upward strokes from the bottom to the top. Check that the entire inside of each dish has been covered with butter before adding a heaped tablespoon of raw cane sugar. Roll and tilt each ramekin so that the sugar coats the inside evenly.

TO MAKE THE MERINGUE: Put half the egg whites into a clean glass or metal bowl. Add the sugar, lemon juice, and salt and whisk until snow white. Add the rest of the egg whites and continue whisking until the meringue forms stiff peaks.

Beat the pastry cream until smooth and then mix in half the meringue until fully incorporated. Gently fold in the rest of the meringue.

Divide the mix between the ramekins and tap the base of each ramekin on the work surface to ensure there are no air pockets. Level the surface of each soufflé by pulling a palette knife (or back edge of a large knife) across the top of the dish, then clean any drips off the outside or they will burn. To help the soufflés rise, run your thumbnail around the top edge of each ramekin to make a groove.

Put the ramekins into the oven immediately and reduce the temperature to 350°F. Bake for 15–20 minutes or until the soufflés have risen by two-thirds of their original size and wobble a little when moved. Serve straightaway.

* Alternative coatings: Mix the sugar with a little ground cinnamon or ginger, or with chile powder (this works particularly well with a chocolate soufflé), or finely grated citrus zest. The sugar can also be replaced with unsweetened cocoa powder.

Preparation time: 40 minutes
Resting time: 1 hour (for the pastry cream) Cooking time: 30 minutes

Mousse aux éclats de chocolat

Chocolate mousse with cocoa nibs

This is for any serious chocaholic. A chocolate *crème Madame* (chocolate pastry cream and whipped cream folded together) makes for an easy and delicious chocolate mousse, but I like something with more of a chocolate attitude.

Each element is vital—chocolate pastry cream for a silky-smooth feel, meringue and whipped cream to make it airy, and melted dark chocolate to give an extra-rich chocolate flavor. I also like to coat my serving glasses with cocoa nibs to add a bitter chocolate crunch. If you can't get hold of cocoa nibs (available at specialty food shops, online, and at some supermarkets), a coating of finely chopped nuts mixed with some cocoa powder is a good alternative.

So this, *Mesdames et Messieurs*, is my ultimate chocolate mousse.

• 2 tbsp soft butter • 1½ oz cocoa nibs, plus extra for serving

For the chocolate meringue: 2 egg whites • ½ cup confectioners' sugar
• a couple of drops of lemon juice • a pinch of salt • 5 oz dark chocolate, finely chopped
• scant 1 cup heavy cream • 1½ cups chilled *Crème Pâtissière* (page 274),
made with 1 tbsp unsweetened cocoa powder instead of vanilla

Brush 4–6 glasses or ramekins with soft butter. Add some cocoa nibs and roll them around the sides and bottom of the glasses until evenly coated.

TO MAKE THE MERINGUE: Put half the egg whites into a clean glass or metal bowl. Add the confectioners' sugar, lemon juice, and salt and whisk until snow white. Add the rest of the egg whites and continue whisking until the meringue forms stiff peaks.

Melt the chocolate in a bain-marie (a heatproof bowl set over a pot of simmering water) or in the microwave on a low setting. Whip the cream to soft peaks.

Beat the pastry cream to remove any lumps before stirring in the melted chocolate. Mix in one-third of the meringue, then gently fold in the rest followed by the whipped cream.

Divide the mousse between the glasses and chill for at least an hour. Serve chilled, sprinkled with cocoa nibs. The mousse is best eaten the same day and should not be kept for more than 2 days (due to the raw egg whites).

Preparation time: 45 minutes Resting time: 2 hours
(including the pastry cream) Cooking time: 35 minutes

Millefeuille aux pommes

Apple millefeuille

Don't be put off by the length of this recipe. It's really quite simple, as it uses ready-made puff pastry and everything can be prepared in advance. In fact, the fillings are best made beforehand to give them time to chill in the fridge. All that's left to do before serving is the assembly.

For the apple compote: 6 dessert apples, peeled and roughly chopped • 1 tbsp Calvados
• 2 tbsp sugar, or more to taste • 1 gelatin sheet (0.07 oz)*

• 3–4 tbsp confectioners' sugar • 8 oz ready-made puff pastry • 2 tbsp butter, melted
• 4 tbsp caraway seeds • 1½ cups chilled *Crème Pâtissière* (page 274)

TO MAKE THE COMPOTE: Cook the apples, Calvados, and sugar in a covered pan on a medium heat for 10 minutes or until the apples are soft. Whizz to a smooth purée in a blender, then taste and add more sugar if needed (don't make it too sweet as the pastry cream is quite sweet). Soak the gelatin in cold water for 10 minutes or until soft. Drain and squeeze out the excess water, then dissolve in the warm apple purée. Refrigerate until cold (it will keep in an airtight container in the fridge for up to a week).

Line a large baking sheet with parchment paper. Dust your rolling pin and work surface with confectioners' sugar. Roll out the pastry to a 12-by-8-inch rectangle ¼ inch thick. Brush with melted butter, dust with confectioners' sugar, and sprinkle with caraway seeds. Dust with 3–4 tablespoons confectioners' sugar a second time and cut into twelve 4-by-2-inch rectangles. Lay the rectangles on the prepared baking sheet and place in the fridge. Preheat the oven to 400°F. Bake the pastry for 20 minutes or until golden, then transfer to a wire rack until cold.

Put the pastry cream and compote into two separate piping bags fitted with small plain nozzles. Start by piping two blobs of pastry cream onto an individual serving plate and sticking a pastry rectangle on top. Pipe two lines of compote on the pastry, then gently place another rectangle over the compote. Pipe two lines of pastry cream on the second rectangle and top with a third rectangle. Repeat to make four millefeuilles altogether. Serve immediately.

* *For a vegetarian version, instead of the gelatin use ½ teaspoon agar powder. Add the powder to the apple purée in a pan and boil for 5 minutes, stirring continuously.*

Other millefeuille ideas

• Chocolate *Crème Pâtissière* (page 274). Replace the caraway seeds with chopped hazelnuts.

• Top the pastry cream with fresh berries. Replace the apple compote with another layer of pastry cream and berries.

Preparation time: 1 hour
Resting time: 2 hours (including pastry cream) Cooking time: 1 hour

Pommes rôties au four avec une sauce béchamel sucrée et épicée

Baked apples with sweet spiced béchamel sauce

Paris, as beautiful as it is, has about the same amount of cold, wet, and gray days as London, although my Parisian friends would hotly dispute this. On those days, curling up on the couch with a steaming bowl of something sweetly spiced is my remedy for the miserable weather. Both spices and sweetness in this recipe can be adapted to your taste, and the sauce can be kept in the fridge for a day or two, ready to be gently reheated when you want it (whisk in a dash of milk if it's become too thick).

• 6 dessert apples • 6 cinnamon sticks

For the sweet béchamel *sauce:* 2 tbsp butter • ¼ cup all-purpose flour
• 2 cups milk, lukewarm • ½ vanilla pod (cut widthwise) • 4 tbsp sugar
• finely grated zest of ¼ orange • ¼ tsp ground ginger
• ½ tsp ground cinnamon • a pinch of nutmeg • 1 clove

Preheat the oven to 300°F. Core each apple and place a cinammon stick in each core. Wrap each apple tightly in parchment paper or aluminum foil and tie with kitchen string. Bake for 15–20 minutes or until the apples are soft but not collapsing.

TO MAKE THE SAUCE: Melt the butter in a large pan over a medium heat. Add the flour and beat hard until you have a smooth paste. Take off the heat and leave to cool for 2 minutes, then gradually add the milk, whisking constantly.

Split the vanilla pod in half lengthwise and scrape out the grains. Place the pan back over a medium heat and add the pod and grains, the sugar, orange zest, and spices. Simmer gently for about 10 minutes, whisking frequently to make sure the sauce doesn't burn on the bottom of the pan. (If the sauce becomes too thick, whisk in a little more milk.) When the sauce is ready, remove the vanilla pod and clove before pouring the sauce into a jug.

Unwrap the apples and stand them upright on individual plates to serve. Let each person take out their cinnamon stick before pouring a generous helping of sauce over the apple.

Preparation time: 15 minutes Baking time: 15–20 minutes

Crème brûlée

Caramel-topped custard

On my first trip to Paris, I ordered a *crème brûlée* and it tasted awful. In my virtually nonexistent French, I tried in vain to complain to the waiter that it tasted burned, only for him to retort that it was *crème brûlée* and meant to be burned. Fortunately now my French is good enough to explain that *crème brûlée* is a rich custard topped with a hard caramel, not a burned caramel.

The classic *crème brûlée* is just cream, egg yolks, sugar, and vanilla, but I use a combination of cream and milk, which makes a rich custard without the heaviness of using only cream. In summer, I often put a small handful of raspberries or blueberries (or a few halved strawberries) into the bottom of each ramekin before completely submerging them in the custard.

• 1¼ cups heavy cream • scant 1 cup milk • 1 vanilla pod • 6 egg yolks • ½ cup sugar

For the caramel topping: 2 tbsp superfine sugar • 2 tbsp raw cane sugar

Pour the cream and milk into a pan. Split the vanilla pod in half lengthwise and scrape out the grains. Add the pod and grains to the cream and milk. Bring to a boil, turn off the heat, and remove the pod from the pan.

Combine the egg yolks with the sugar in a bowl, then slowly pour in the hot cream, whisking continuously. Do not overwhisk as you want to avoid creating too many bubbles.

If you have time, pour the custard into a bowl, cover with plastic wrap, and refrigerate overnight. This gives the vanilla more time to flavor the cream and milk.

Preheat the oven to 225°F. Divide the custard between six wide, shallow ramekins and place in a roasting pan. Pour cold water into the pan to come halfway up the ramekins. Bake for 30–40 minutes or until the custard is set around the edges but still slightly wobbly in the middle. Remove the ramekins from the water and set aside until cooled to room temperature. Cover the ramekins with plastic wrap (don't let it touch the custard) and refrigerate for at least 4 hours, or overnight.

WHEN READY TO SERVE, MAKE THE CARAMEL TOPPING: Uncover the ramekins and check to see if condensation has collected on the custards. If it has, gently place paper towels on the surface to soak up the moisture. Mix the two types of sugar together and sprinkle a nice even layer of sugar over each custard. Do this by holding the spoon at least 12 inches away from the ramekin—sprinkling from a height is the best way to create an even layer of sugar. »»»

Place the ramekins on a metal tray. For best results, use a handheld blowtorch and hold it 4–5 inches away from the sugar. Move the flame slowly around the sugar, maintaining a slow and even motion. Stop torching just before the desired degree of caramelization is reached, as the sugar will continue to cook for a few seconds after the flame has been removed.

If you don't have a blowtorch, take a large metal spoon and hold it in a gas flame until very hot (it will turn blue, almost black in color). Place the spoon on the sugar and move it around so that the heat of the spoon caramelizes the sugar.

Why not try something different instead of vanilla?

The key is to add dry ingredients or just a teaspoon or two of liquid flavoring (e.g., almond extract, orange flower water, rose water) to the cream and milk before bringing to a boil—any more liquid and there's a risk of the custard not setting. Here are some ideas.

- *1 teaspoon dried lavender (strain it out before combining the cream and milk with the egg yolks and sugar)*
- *finely grated zest of 1 orange or lemon*
- *½ teaspoon ground cinnamon and ¼ teaspoon ground ginger*
- *½ teaspoon freshly ground black pepper or Indonesian long pepper (this goes particularly well with raspberries in the crème brûlée)*
- *a pinch of saffron threads*

Tips

- *The custard can be made up to 4 days in advance, but the caramel topping has to be done just before serving. Caramel becomes soft with time, due to the humidity in the air.*
- *You need wide, shallow ramekins to get a high caramel to custard ratio, which is key for a successful crème brûlée.*
- *If you're not using the leftover egg whites straightaway, freeze them in an airtight container with the date on the label and use within a month. They can also be kept in the fridge for several days.*

Preparation time: 20 minutes Baking time: 30–40 minutes
Resting time: 4 hours–overnight

Crème caramel

Vanilla cream with caramel sauce

I loved this dessert when I was a kid—French food wasn't very common at home. Growing up in the United Kingdom with an Austrian mother and a Malay–Chinese dad meant that meals were a fusion of Alpine sweetness and Southeast Asian spiciness, with a traditional British roast on Sundays. My mother's version of *crème caramel* was courtesy of a powdered mix and it didn't bother me at all. Considering how simple it is to make, nowadays I prefer the real deal.

For the caramel sauce: 1¼ cups sugar

• **2 cups milk** • **1 vanilla pod** • **⅓ cup sugar** • **3 eggs plus 2 egg yolks** • **half-and-half, to serve**

TO MAKE THE CARAMEL SAUCE: Sprinkle a thin layer of sugar over the bottom of a heavy-based pan and place on a medium heat. Once the sugar starts to melt, add some more. Repeat several times until all the sugar has melted. Continue heating the caramel, swirling it around in the pan (do not stir).* When the caramel is almost a Coca-Cola color, add a couple of tablespoons of water (stand back a little as it may splatter). Pour some caramel into a ramekin and immediately swirl it all over the bottom of the dish. Repeat with five more ramekins, working very fast as the caramel sets quickly. Set the ramekins aside while you make the cream.

Preheat the oven to 225°F. Pour the milk into a pan. Split the vanilla pod lengthwise and scrape out the grains. Add the pod and grains to the milk and bring to a boil. Remove from the heat and take out the pod. Combine the eggs, egg yolks, and sugar in a bowl, then slowly pour in the hot milk, whisking continuously. Do not overwhisk as you want to avoid creating too many bubbles.

Divide the mixture between the ramekins and place in a roasting pan. Pour cold water into the pan to come halfway up the sides of the ramekins. Bake for 30–40 minutes or until the cream is set around the edges but still slightly wobbly in the middle. Remove the ramekins from the water and set aside until cooled to room temperature. Cover with plastic wrap (don't let it touch the custard), and refrigerate for at least 4 hours, or overnight.

Run a knife around the top edge of the cream and dip each ramekin in boiling water for about 30 seconds. Invert a plate on top of the ramekin, then turn both over and give them a shake or two to release the vanilla cream and caramel sauce onto the plate. Serve chilled, with a jug of half-and-half.

* **Pourquoi?** *Using a spoon to stir the caramel will agitate the sugar molecules and make the caramel crystallize.*

Preparation time: 20 minutes Baking time: 30–40 minutes
Resting time: 4 hours–overnight

Iles flottantes

Floating islands

Iles flottantes are the perfect finish to any rich meal. Egg whites are whisked into the lightest meringue and gently poached, then floated on a lake of creamy, cold *crème anglaise* and topped with praline.

Crème anglaise is one of the all-time classic French dessert sauces and a great one to have under your belt. Once you understand the technique, you'll be able to adapt the recipe with your own flavorings. I like to add some freshly ground long pepper, which is sweet and spicy and gives the whole thing a little kick. (You're most likely to find long pepper at an Asian super-market, or it can be replaced with regular black pepper.)

This dessert should be served cold, which makes it perfect for preparing in advance. The praline can be made a couple of weeks before you need it and the *crème anglaise* a couple of days ahead. Keep the praline in an airtight container, as humidity will make it soggy and sticky. The meringues are best made on the day of serving.

For the crème anglaise: 4 egg yolks • 7 tbsp sugar • 1 vanilla pod* • 2 cups milk
• ½ tsp ground long pepper or black pepper (optional)

For the praline: 6½ tbsp sugar • scant 1 tbsp water • ½ cup slivered almonds

For the islands: 2 egg whites • scant ½ cup confectioners' sugar, sifted if lumpy
• a couple of drops of lemon juice • a pinch of salt

TO MAKE THE *CRÈME ANGLAISE:* Mix the egg yolks and sugar together in a bowl. Split the vanilla pod in half lengthwise and scrape out the grains. Place the pod and grains in a pan with the milk and pepper and bring to a boil. Remove the pod, then pour a little of the hot milk onto the egg yolks and sugar, whisking continuously. Gradually whisk in the rest of the milk, then pour the mix into a clean pan, set over a gentle heat, and whisk constantly. Do not let the custard simmer at any point or it will split. After 5 minutes it will begin to thicken slightly and become the consistency of half-and-half (it will thicken more when it cools down). Transfer to a bowl and chill in the fridge for at least 4 hours.

MEANWHILE, MAKE THE PRALINE: Line a baking sheet with parchment paper. Put the sugar and water into a large pan, heat gently until the sugar dissolves, then increase the heat to high. When the mixture starts to bubble, add the almonds and stir continuously for 5 minutes to prevent them from sticking to the bottom of the pan and burning. Once the sugar and nuts have become a dark golden caramel color, pour onto the prepared sheet and spread as thinly as possible with a palette knife (be quick as it sets pretty fast). Leave to cool.   »»»

TO MAKE THE ISLANDS: Put half the egg whites into a clean glass or metal bowl. Add the sugar, lemon juice, and salt and whisk until snow white. Add the rest of the egg whites and continue whisking until the meringue forms stiff peaks.

Gently drop six spoonfuls of meringue into a large pot of simmering water** and simmer for a few minutes or until they are slightly puffed up and just set. Remove with a slotted spoon and place on a sheet of parchment paper until needed.

Pour a ladleful of *crème anglaise* into each of six glasses and gently place a meringue in the center. Snap the praline into small pieces and sprinkle on top.

 * *The vanilla pod can be interchanged with different flavorings. Here are a few ideas to get your imagination going.*

Winter warming: *1 cinnamon stick, ½ teaspoon ground ginger, and a pinch of nutmeg*

Chocolate chile: *4 tablespoons unsweetened cocoa powder and 2 pinches of chile powder, or to taste*

Zingy citrus fruit: *finely grated zest of 1 orange, ½ lemon, and ½ lime*

** *If you prefer you can cook the islands in the microwave. Spoon six small heaps onto a plate, leaving at least ¾ inch between each one, and microwave on medium-high for 30–60 seconds.*

Preparation time: 45 minutes Resting time: 4 hours
Cooking time: 30 minutes

Mont blanc

Meringue and chestnut-cream mountain

With only three main ingredients—meringue, whipped cream, and sweetened chestnut cream—there's really not much to this dessert. And if you're short of time, you could even get away with buying the ingredients ready-made and just assembling them before serving.

Traditionally the chestnut cream should be thick enough to be piped, but I like mine a little runnier, so that I can pour it over the meringues and cream to make them look like mini mountains—hence the name Mont Blanc.

For the meringues: 3 egg whites • ⅔ cup confectioners' sugar
• a couple of drops of lemon juice • a pinch of salt

For the chestnut cream: 1 vanilla pod • 7 oz cooked chestnuts (from a can is fine)
• 1 cup heavy cream • 2 tbsp golden superfine sugar • 1½ tbsp Cognac (optional)

To assemble: ¾ cup plus 2 tbsp heavy cream

TO MAKE THE MERINGUES: Preheat the oven to 175°F and line a baking sheet with parchment paper. Put half the egg whites into a clean glass or metal bowl. Add the sugar, lemon juice, and salt and whisk until snow white. Add the rest of the egg whites and continue whisking until the meringue forms stiff peaks.

Spoon four heaped peaks of meringue onto the prepared pan (ideally they should look like mini mountains). Bake for 2 hours or until crisp, opening the oven door a few times to release any steam. Remove them from the paper and leave to cool on a wire rack. (Once cold, the meringues can be kept in an airtight container for a good couple of days.)

TO MAKE THE CHESTNUT CREAM: Split the vanilla pod in half lengthwise and scrape out the grains. Put the pod and grains into a pot with the rest of the ingredients and bring to a simmer on a medium heat. Simmer for 10 minutes or until the chestnuts are soft and slightly mushy. Remove the vanilla pod and whizz the chestnuts to a soft, creamy purée in a blender. Chill until needed (it will keep for up to a week in an airtight container).

TO ASSEMBLE: Whip the cream to soft peaks. Place the meringues on individual plates, spoon over the whipped cream, and pour over the chestnut cream (if it has set too thick, whisk in some heavy cream). Serve straightaway.

Preparation time: 30 minutes Resting time: 1 hour
Baking time: 2 hours

Vacherin "hot dog" avec rhubarbe au romarin

Vacherin "hot dog" with rosemary rhubarb

A *vacherin* dessert is not to be confused with the gooey, pungent cheese of the same name. Apart from the name and shape, they have little else in common. The dessert is composed of large meringue disks layered with whipped cream and fruit. It looks stunning until you try and cut it, when it turns into meringue-and-cream carnage. I find it easier to make individual portions, and I also think it's fun to pipe the meringues and sandwich them together with rhubarb and cream to resemble hot dogs.

For the compote: 2–3 stalks of rhubarb • 7 tbsp superfine sugar • 1 sprig of rosemary

For the meringue: 2 egg whites • ½ cup confectioners' sugar
• a couple of drops of lemon juice • a pinch of salt

To assemble: ¾ cup plus 2 tbsp heavy cream

TO MAKE THE COMPOTE: Trim the rhubarb and cut the stalks into eight pieces, each about 4 inches long. Put the sugar and rosemary into a pan over a medium heat and heat until the sugar has melted. Add the rhubarb and reduce the heat to low, then cover and cook gently for 5–10 minutes or until the rhubarb is tender but still holds its shape. Leave to cool, then remove the rosemary. (The rhubarb tastes better if it's cooked at least a day in advance and it can be kept in the fridge for up to a week.)

TO MAKE THE MERINGUE: Preheat the oven to 175°F and line a baking sheet with parchment paper. Put half the egg whites into a clean glass or metal bowl. Add the sugar, lemon juice, and salt and whisk until snow white. Add the rest of the egg whites and continue whisking until the meringue forms stiff peaks.

Spoon the meringue into a piping bag fitted with a ⅜-inch nozzle and pipe eight 4-inch-long strips onto the prepared pan. Bake for 2 hours or until crisp, opening the oven door a few times to release any steam. Remove the meringues from the paper and leave to cool on a wire rack. (Once cold, they can be kept in an airtight container for a good couple of days.)

TO ASSEMBLE: Whip the cream to stiff peaks and spoon into a piping bag fitted with a ¼-inch nozzle. Lift the rhubarb out of its juice and drain well. Pipe a line of cream on the flat side of two pieces of meringue and sandwich two pieces of rhubarb between them. Repeat to make four hot dogs and serve straightaway.

Preparation time: 30–45 minutes   Baking time: 2 hours

Tartlets aux framboises et amandes

Raspberry and almond tartlets

When I tell French people that I studied and now teach *pâtisserie*, their eyes often light up. One friend was so impressed with these tartlets that he nicknamed me Tartlet. Translated as "little tart," this may sound rather dubious, but in French it doesn't have the same connotation.

• 6 tbsp soft butter • 1 tsp sugar • a pinch of salt
• 1⅓ cups all-purpose flour • 2 egg yolks • 2 tbsp ice-cold water

For the almond cream: 2 cups ground almonds • 1 cup sugar • scant 1 cup soft butter • 2 eggs

• 10 oz raspberries*

Using a wooden spoon, beat together the butter, sugar, and salt until soft and creamy. Mix in the flour followed by the egg yolks and ice-cold water. Bring together to make a smooth ball, adding a little more water if the pastry is too crumbly (only knead as much as necessary to bring the dough together). Wrap the dough in plastic wrap and refrigerate for a minimum of an hour (best overnight).

TO MAKE THE CREAM: Beat the almonds, sugar, and butter just until smooth, then beat in the eggs.

Remove the pastry from the fridge 30 minutes before using and preheat the oven to 350°F. Roll out the pastry between two sheets of parchment paper until ⅛–¼ inch thick. Cut out four rectangles of pastry large enough to line four 4½-by-2½-inch tartlet pans with a ¾-inch overhang.** Place the pastry in the pans and prick each base several times with a fork. Spread the almond cream in the pastry shells and arrange the raspberries on top, keeping them close together so that they almost cover the cream. Trim off the pastry overhang.

Bake for 15–20 minutes or until the pastry edges are golden brown. Best eaten warm. Cold is fine too (but not refrigerated).

* *Any kind of fruit works, even canned and frozen (thawed), as long as it's drained of excess liquid.*

** *If you prefer, you can make six round tartlets in 4-inch tartlet pans, or one large 9-inch tart. The baking time for the large tart will be 30 minutes.*

Preparation time: 20 minutes Resting time: 1 hour–overnight
Baking time: 15–20 minutes

Tarte Tatin

Upside-down apple tart

In the late-nineteenth century, the Tatin sisters came up with this great recipe at their restaurant in Lamotte-Beuvron in the Sologne. It was all an accident, apparently. They burned their apple tart and decided to remove the burned pastry at the bottom, keep the caramelized apples, and put new pastry on the top. Who said that accidents can't be a good thing in the kitchen?

My version has the pastry baked separately instead of over the apples. This way, the pastry stays crisp rather than going soggy.

The traditional *tarte Tatin* calls for a classic caramel sauce but I like to make a salted caramel sauce, which is typically Breton, and serve with ice cream or a dollop of crème fraîche.

For the salted caramel: • ½ cup sugar • 4 tbsp soft butter • 1 tsp salt

• 8 oz puff pastry • 14–16 dessert apples • 2 tbsp butter, melted • sugar, for sprinkling

TO MAKE THE SALTED CARAMEL: Sprinkle a thin layer of the sugar over the bottom of a heavy-based pan and place on a medium heat. Once the sugar starts to melt, add some more of the sugar. Repeat a couple of times until all the sugar has melted. Continue heating the caramel, swirling it around in the pan (do not stir). When the caramel is almost a Coca-Cola color, take the pan off the heat and swirl in the butter (stand back a little as it may splatter) and add the salt. Pour the caramel into the tart pan and swirl it around to cover the bottom and sides.

Preheat the oven to 350°F. Roll out the pastry on a floured surface until it is ⅜ inch thick and cut out a disk that is about ⅛ inch bigger than a 10-inch round tart pan. Place the pastry on a baking sheet and prick all over with a fork. Bake for 30 minutes or until the pastry is puffy and golden.

Peel, core, and halve the apples. Sit them tightly upright in the tart pan, making sure they are really snug (they shrink when they cook). You can cut the last apple into quarters to stuff some of the large holes. Brush the apples with the melted butter and sprinkle some sugar on top. Bake for 30 minutes or until the apples are tender but not mushy. Remove from the oven and leave the apples to cool until they are not too hot to the touch.

Place the pastry on top of the apples, then invert a large dinner plate on top of the pastry. Turn the tart and the plate over so that the apples come out on top of the pastry. Serve straightaway.

Preparation time: 30 minutes Baking time: 1 hour
Resting time: 30 minutes

Moelleux au chocolat

Chocolate lava cake

Cook'n with Class is a little cookery school in Montmartre where I used to teach French *pâtisserie*. The students are a pretty international crowd, from young backpackers and honeymooners to pensioners, but they all have a few classic dessert recipes that they would like to learn. One of the top-ten favorites is *moelleux au chocolat*.

Moelleux means "soft" or "tender," which perfectly describes this dessert. Like a volcano, the cake has a center that explodes when you dive in with your spoon. Pair with vanilla ice cream, whipped cream, or fresh berries.

Special thanks for this recipe to Eric Fraudeau, the owner at Cook'n with Class.

- **2 tbsp soft butter, plus ¾ cup butter, cubed • 6 tbsp unsweetened cocoa powder**
- **6 oz dark chocolate, finely chopped • ¾ cup light brown sugar**
- **⅔ cup all-purpose flour • 6 eggs, beaten**

Prepare 6–8 ramekins by brushing them with the soft butter and then dusting with the cocoa powder. Make sure to tap out all the excess cocoa powder.

Melt the chocolate with the cubed butter in a bain-marie (a heatproof bowl set over a pan of simmering water), stirring occasionally. Alternatively, melt them in the microwave on a low setting.

Combine the brown sugar and flour in a bowl. Mix the melted chocolate with the eggs followed by the flour and sugar. Divide the mixture between the ramekins and refrigerate for a minimum of 1 hour.*

Preheat the oven to 350°F. Bake the cakes for 15–20 minutes or until the edges are firm and the centers slightly runny. Test by inserting a toothpick in the center—it should come out wet. Leave to rest for 2 minutes before turning the cakes out of the ramekins onto plates. Serve immediately.

* Pourquoi? Baking your batter from cold will make it slower for the heat from the oven to penetrate the middle of the cakes, which will make the centers all the more gooey. The ramekins filled with the batter can be covered with plastic wrap (don't let it touch the batter) and kept in the fridge for several days. They can also be well wrapped in plastic wrap and frozen, then baked from frozen (they will need an extra 5–10 minutes in the oven—test to see if they are done as above).

Preparation time: 20 minutes Resting time: 1 hour
Baking time: 15–20 minutes

Moelleux au chocolat coeur fondant caramel salé

Chocolate lava cake with salted caramel filling

At Cook'n with Class they tend to keep *moelleux au chocolat* simple and serve it just as it comes, but when I'm at home I like to pipe a little salted caramel filling into the center, which makes it even harder to say *non* to this dessert. The salted caramel recipe makes a little more than you need for the *moelleux au chocolat*, but it's good with virtually anything—on toast, ice cream, stirred into plain yogurt . . .

For the salted caramel filling:* ¾ cup sugar • ⅔ cup heavy cream
• 1 tsp *fleur de sel* or coarse sea salt

TO MAKE THE CARAMEL FILLING: Sprinkle a thin layer of sugar over the bottom of a heavy-bottomed pan and place on a medium heat. Once the sugar starts to melt, add some more sugar. Repeat a couple of times until all the sugar has melted. Continue heating the caramel, swirling it around in the pan (do not stir**). When the caramel is almost a Coca-Cola color, add the cream and salt (be careful as the caramel may splatter). Cook until the temperature reaches 226°F, or until the caramel coats the back of a spoon, then pour into a dish and leave to cool a little.

Follow the main recipe for *moelleux au chocolat*, but only fill the ramekins three-quarters full with the chocolate mixture.

Once the caramel is cool, transfer it to a piping bag fitted with a small round nozzle, or to a heavy-duty food bag (just snip off the corner to use). Pop the piping nozzle into the middle of the chocolate mixture in each ramekin and squirt in the filling (the mixture will rise almost to the top).

Bake and serve as for *moelleux au chocolat*.

* *For an alternative fruit filling, warm ⅔ cup jam (raspberry, orange, mango . . .) in a pan or in the microwave until runny, then whizz in a blender until smooth. Leave to cool before piping into the rame-kins as for the salted caramel filling.*

** ***Pourquoi?*** *Using a spoon to stir the caramel will agitate the sugar molecules and make the caramel crystallize*

Preparation time: 30 minutes Resting time: 1 hour
Baking time: 15–20 minutes

Sabayon de Champagne avec fraises gariguettes et tomates cerises

Champagne sabayon with strawberries and cherry tomatoes

According to scientists, strawberries and tomatoes should be interchangeable in recipes as they share the same flavor components, and I think my little scientific experiment has turned out pretty well, adding a modern twist to this classic recipe.

Like the English, the French love their strawberries, and one of the most popular varieties is the Gariguette. Elongated and conical in shape, with a delicate sweet flavor, the berries are delicious eaten on their own or in this light and fluffy dish.

For the sabayon: 4 egg yolks • 2 tbsp sugar • 6½ tbsp Champagne

• 7 oz strawberries (Gariguettes if you can get them), halved or quartered
• 3½ oz cherry tomatoes, quartered and seeded

TO MAKE THE SABAYON: Put the egg yolks and sugar into a bain-marie (a heatproof bowl set over a pan of simmering water) and whisk until pale yellow and thick. Add the Champagne and continue whisking until the sabayon is very thick and foamy, about 10 minutes. To test, draw a figure eight in the mixture with the whisk; if the figure stays put, then the sabayon is ready.

Divide the sabayon between four bowls, place the strawberries and tomatoes on top, and serve straightaway. Alternatively, chill the sabayon until ready to use (a couple of hours is fine) and add the strawberries and tomatoes just before serving.

Preparation time: 10 minutes Cooking time: 10–15 minutes

Poires Belle Hélène

Beautiful Helen pears

In the late-nineteenth century, Auguste Escoffier found inspiration for this recipe in Offenbach's operetta *La Belle Hélène*. The beauty of the dish lies in its simplicity: pears poached in a sugar syrup, served cold with a warm chocolate sauce. I've added cardamom to the chocolate sauce, which gives it a lovely warmth. Serve with a scoop of vanilla ice cream or a dollop of whipped cream.

• 6½ cups cold water • 1 vanilla pod • ¾ cup sugar
• 4 firm pears (e.g., Bartlett), peeled with stems still attached

For the cardamom chocolate sauce: 3½ oz dark or white chocolate, finely chopped
• 7 tbsp heavy cream • 3 cardamom pods, crushed

Pour the water into a large pan. Split the vanilla pod in half lengthwise and scrape out the grains. Add the pod and grains to the water with the sugar and bring to a simmer, stirring occasionally to dissolve the sugar. Add the pears and place a piece of parchment paper on top to keep them submerged, then simmer gently for 20 minutes. Insert a skewer or small sharp knife to test whether the pears are tender. If not, simmer for another 5 minutes. When the pears are cooked, leave them to cool in the syrup for at least a couple of hours, preferably overnight, to give them time to take on the flavor of the vanilla. (They can be kept in an airtight container in the fridge for a couple of days.)

TO MAKE THE SAUCE: Put the chocolate into a bowl. Bring the cream to a boil with the crushed cardamom pods and pour over the chocolate. Leave to stand for a minute until the chocolate has melted, remove the cardamom pods (leaving the seeds behind in the sauce), then stir the sauce gently until smooth. Do not overmix or the chocolate may split—the cocoa solids will separate from the cocoa butter. (The sauce can be made in advance and reheated very gently in the microwave or a bain-marie.)

To serve, remove the pears from the syrup* and stand them upright on individual plates. Pour a generous helping of chocolate sauce over them.

* Keep the sugar syrup in the fridge and use for fruit salads.

Preparation time: 20 minutes Resting time: 2 hours–overnight
Cooking time: 30 minutes

Fontainebleau avec un coulis de carotte et cannelle

Fontainebleau with a carrot cinnamon coulis

Unlike the *château* of the same name, the dessert *fontainebleau* is not elaborate. Whipped cream, *fromage blanc*, sugar, and vanilla are simply mixed together and pressed. It makes for a wonderful light ending to a meal and is especially refreshing when served with a cold fruit sauce or a handful of berries—or in this case, with a carrot and cinnamon coulis.

For the coulis: 3 carrots, grated • ⅔ cup carrot juice • juice of 1 orange
• 1 tbsp sugar • a pinch of ground cinnamon

• ½ vanilla pod (cut widthwise) • ¾ cup plus 1 tbsp heavy cream • 1 tsp sugar
• 7 oz *fromage blanc* or Quark • ground cinnamon, to serve

TO MAKE THE COULIS: Put all the ingredients into a pot, cover, and bring to a simmer. Cook for 10 minutes and then whizz to a smooth purée in a blender. Chill in the fridge until serving time.

Split the vanilla pod in half lengthwise and scrape out the grains. Put the grains into a bowl with the cream and sugar and whisk to stiff peaks. Fold the cream into the *fromage blanc*.

Line a large colander with a clean tea towel and stand the colander in a large bowl. Put the cream mix into the colander and enclose in the tea towel, tying the ends together tightly to make a parcel. Place a heavy pot (you can add water to make it heavier) on top of the tea towel and refrigerate overnight or up to 24 hours.

To serve, pour the chilled coulis into 4–6 bowls, add a generous scoop of *fontainebleau* to each bowl, and sprinkle with a pinch of cinnamon.

Preparation time: 30 minutes Resting time: overnight–24 hours
Cooking time: 10 minutes

Riz rouge au lait d'amande

Red rice pudding with almond milk

There is something creamy and comforting about *riz au lait* that brings back childhood memories for most French people. It's traditionally made with short-grain white rice, milk, and cream, but I also like it with red rice from the Camargue (in the south of France). This gives the pudding a fabulous color as well as a subtle nuttiness, which is accentuated by the almond milk. I'm not shy of piling on a few more calories, so I serve it with *crème Chantilly*.

• rounded ¾ cup red rice • 2 cups unsweetened almond milk* • ½ tsp almond extract

For the crème Chantilly: ½ vanilla pod (cut widthwise)
• ⅔ cup heavy cream • 4 tbsp sugar

• 2 tbsp sugar, or to taste

Put the rice, almond milk, and almond extract into a large pan and bring to a gentle simmer. Cover and simmer gently for 25–30 minutes or until the rice is tender but still slightly nutty in texture. Stir occasionally to make sure the rice doesn't stick to the bottom of the pan.

MEANWHILE, MAKE THE *CRÈME CHANTILLY*: Split the vanilla pod in half lengthwise and scrape out the grains. Put the grains in a bowl with the cream and sugar and whisk to stiff peaks.

Add the sugar to the rice and serve the pudding either warm or chilled,** topped with the *crème Chantilly*.

 * *You can buy almond milk at some large supermarkets, health food shops, and online.*
** *Once cool, chill the rice in a covered container in the fridge for about 4 hours (it will keep for a couple of days). You may need to add a little more almond milk to loosen up the rice before serving.*

Preparation time: 5 minutes Cooking time: 30 minutes

Tartlets au pamplemousse et poire meringuées

Grapefruit and pepper meringue tartlets

Unlike the tartlets on page 245, these use a traditional Breton biscuit recipe for the base*. It's a great alternative to classic pastry as there's no need to chill or roll out the dough. I like to add some freshly ground black pepper to my meringue. It may sound odd, but the little spicy kick works really well with the acidity of the grapefruit curd.

For the grapefruit curd: **1** grapefruit • **½** cup sugar • a pinch of salt • **1** egg plus **1** egg yolk
• **1** heaped tbsp cornstarch • **4** tbsp soft butter, cubed

For the biscuit base: **5½** tbsp butter, very soft but not melted • **6** tbsp sugar
• a generous pinch of salt • finely grated zest of **½** lemon • **2** egg yolks
• **¾** cup all-purpose flour • **2** tsp baking powder

*For the Italian meringue:*** **½** cup sugar • **2½** tbsp water • **2** egg whites
• a pinch of salt • **½** tsp pepper

TO MAKE THE GRAPEFRUIT CURD: Finely grate the zest of the grapefruit and squeeze the juice. Measure 6 tablespoons juice into a pan and whisk together with the zest, sugar, salt, and eggs over a gentle heat. Sift in the cornstarch and continue to whisk. Don't stop whisking at any point, otherwise the eggs will curdle. Once the curd is as thick as puréed tomatoes and has released a bubble or two, take it off the heat and whisk in the butter a cube at a time. Pour into a bowl and place plastic wrap in direct contact with the curd. Refrigerate for at least an hour (best overnight).

TO MAKE THE BISCUIT BASE: Preheat the oven to 350°F and butter six 3¼-by-2-inch metal dessert rings. Cream together the butter and sugar with the salt and lemon zest until fluffy and pale in color. Add the egg yolks and continue to beat. Sift the flour and baking powder together, add to the creamed mixture, and continue beating until the dough comes together as a smooth paste. Put the dough into a piping bag fitted with a ⅜-inch round nozzle. »»

Pipe the dough into the rings to come about ⅛ inch high, then use a spoon dipped in hot water to level out the pastry. Bake for 12–15 minutes or until golden (but not too dark).*** Leave to cool for a couple of minutes before running a small sharp knife around the inside of each ring to release the biscuit. Transfer the biscuits to a wire rack (be careful as they're fragile) and leave to cool.

TO MAKE THE ITALIAN MERINGUE: Put the sugar into a pan with the water and place on a high heat. Bring to the soft-ball stage (245°F on a sugar thermometer), which will take about 10 minutes. To test without a thermometer, drop a tiny bit of sugar syrup into a bowl of very cold water. If it forms a soft sticky ball right away, it is ready.

While waiting for the sugar syrup, start whisking the egg whites with the salt and pepper in a glass or metal bowl. Do not whisk to soft peaks, just a light froth. Once the sugar syrup has reached the soft-ball stage, beat the egg whites on high speed at the same time as pouring the syrup onto them in a thin stream. (Don't pour the syrup over the whisk, but down the side of the bowl.) Continue to whisk for 10 minutes or until the egg whites are glossy and stiff.

Spread the grapefruit curd on top of the biscuits followed by the meringue. Either place under a very hot broiler for a couple of minutes or use a blowtorch to brown. Serve immediately.

* *The bases can be eaten on their own as Breton biscuits. They will keep in an airtight container for up to a week.*

**Pourquoi? *In French* pâtisserie *there are three types of meringue:*

French—The best-known meringue, for which egg whites are simply whisked with sugar. It is also the least stable as the egg whites are not cooked while being whisked. Best baked immediately or the egg whites begin to deflate. Used in desserts like vacherin and Mont Blanc, and eaten on their own (like the ones you see in *pâtisserie* windows).

Swiss—Egg whites are whisked with sugar over a bain-marie, then taken off and whisked until cool and stiff. This technique ensures that the sugar is completely dissolved and makes a very firm meringue. Used for icing and baked decorations (piped into different shapes such as mushrooms or flowers).

Italian—Egg whites are whisked while a hot sugar syrup is poured onto them. This cooks the egg whites, making a stable and stiff meringue. Used for topping cakes and desserts and for making macarons. It is best made using a stand mixer or a powerful handheld mixer.

*** *Instead of six tartlets you can make one large tart in a 10-inch tart pan. The baking time will be 30– 40 minutes.*

Preparation time: 1 hour Resting time: 1 hour–overnight
Cooking time: 30 minutes

Sélection de fromage avec une confiture de tomates cerises et vanille

Cheese selection with cherry tomato and vanilla jam

For me, cheese, wine, and a crusty baguette are the perfect *ménage à trois*. But which cheese? There are more than two hundred different French cheeses to choose from, and it's no wonder that Charles de Gaulle said, "How can anyone govern a nation that has 246 different kinds of cheese?"

It can be quite daunting to know what to choose, but nowadays there are no set rules. You can get away with serving just one excellent cheese rather than three mediocre ones.

In France many cheeses have the AOC *(appellation d'origine contrôlée)* label. This means that the product's origin is protected and strict guidelines are enforced. (Probably the most commonly known AOC is that of Champagne—sparkling wine produced in the Champagne region is the only one to be allowed the name.)

If you are serving more than one cheese, it's best to start with the mildest so that its flavor is not overpowered by a stronger cheese—i.e., on a cheese board, a mild goat's cheese would be the first and a blue cheese the last.

There's an art to everything in France and this applies to cutting cheese as much as anything else. Without getting too technical, a general rule of thumb is that every portion of cheese should include some of the rind (the flavor gets stronger closer to the rind).

When trying to match wine with cheese, it can help to choose a wine produced in the same region as the cheese, e.g., a glass of Calvados (apple liqueur) is a good match with Camembert as they both come from Normandy.

As a general guideline, go by the texture and taste of the cheese rather than the smell. A soft and creamy cheese is equally good with a sweet, soft wine as it is with a tangy acidic wine, whereas strong or salty cheeses normally go best with an acidic wine. Remember, the more mature and salty the cheese, the more aggressive the taste when it is eaten with wine.

The wines listed with the cheeses on the following pages are only suggestions, so don't feel that they are the only ones you can drink with that cheese. At the end of the day, it's all a matter of personal taste.

It's impossible to mention every French cheese, so I've just listed some of the classics that I like and that are easy to find. Should you be lucky enough to have a local *fromagerie*, do try out some of the cheeses that are less well known. 　　　　　　　　　　　　　　　　**»»»**

Selles-sur-Cher

A goat's cheese that is covered with a layer of charcoal. The rind is meant to be eaten and contributes to the overall flavor, which is slightly acidic and salty with a melt-in-the-mouth mildness. It has a delicate hazelnut aftertaste.

Wine: Sancerre, Pouilly Fumé

Crottin de Chavignol

This goat's cheese is best eaten after it has matured for a minimum of 2 weeks, when it gets a fine layer of blue and white mold and loses some of its moisture. (Otherwise, according to the French, it's not a real *crottin.*) The older it gets, the more crumbly, hard, and salty it becomes. When slightly warmed, it is delicious with a simple green salad.

Wine: Sancerre

Brie de Meaux

Produced about 30 miles east of Paris, this cow's milk cheese is a popular choice on Parisian cheese boards. It has a light, straw-colored, and velvety soft rind and is slightly creamier and milder than its Normandy cousin, Camembert. There's also *Brie noir* that is matured for up to a year, making it a lot denser and drier than the regular brie, which is usually matured for 4–6 weeks. The traditional way of eating *Brie noir* is to dip it into your coffee at breakfast.

Wine: Saint-Julien, Champagne

Comté

What Cheddar is for the English, Comté is for the French—probably the most popular hard cheese. The best Comté is sold according to its maturing age of 12 months, 18 months, or 36 months. The 36-month version often develops salt crystals and is similar in strength to Parmesan. Comté is a cheese that can be used for most things, from sandwiches and soufflés to gratins.

Wine: Côtes du Jura

Morbier

This cow's milk cheese has a thin blue line running through the middle. It was developed by farmers who had morning milk left over from making Comté and sprinkled it with a layer of ash to protect it. The leftover evening milk was then poured on top, and during the maturing process the charcoal developed into a blue mold, giving the cheese its characteristic look and taste.

Wine: Crépy (Savoie)

Camembert

The little village of Camembert in Normandy gives this famous quite pungent, soft cheese its name. The cheese is ripe when it is soft to touch (it shouldn't be firm), has a creamy yellow color, and a light "moldy" smell. There are some Camembert varieties that have their rinds brushed with cider or Calvados.

Wine: Saint-Émilion (or Calvados)

Roquefort

After Comté, Roquefort comes in second as the most popular cheese for the French. In 1411, the French king Charles VI granted the inhabitants of the village of Roquefort a monopoly on the production of the famous blue cheese. Roquefort can be extremely strong (eat it last if it is on a cheese board with other cheeses), which means a little goes a long way. Due to the slight aggressiveness of the cheese, it is best matched with a sweet wine or one without acidic notes.

Wine: Sauternes

Compotée de tomates cerises et vanille

Cherry tomato and vanilla compote

Marie is the only French friend I know who makes her own jam, sourdough bread, and yogurt. So what better person to ask for a little something to go with cheese? She recommends eating this compote with an aged goat's cheese like *crottin de Chavignol* or a fresh goat's cheese.

• 1 lb cherry tomatoes of various shapes • a generous pinch of salt
• 3 tbsp sugar • 3 tbsp light olive oil • 1 vanilla pod

Wash and dry the tomatoes and cut them in half. Arrange skin-side down on a large nonstick baking sheet and sprinkle with the salt and sugar. Set aside at room temperature while you get on with the vanilla oil.

Put the olive oil into a small bowl. Cut the vanilla pod in half lengthwise and scrape out the grains. Using a teaspoon, mix the grains with the olive oil. Add the vanilla pod and infuse for 15 minutes.

Preheat the oven to 250°F.

Pour the infused oil (plus the vanilla pod) over the tomatoes and slow roast for 50–60 minutes, checking regularly. Once cooked, the tomatoes will still be red, but some will be very slightly brown.

Serve lukewarm or cold. (The compote will keep for a couple of days in the fridge. Once cool, transfer to a glass jar, scraping the baking sheet for extra caramel, and cover with a tight-fitting lid.)

Preparation time: 20 minutes Resting time: 15 minutes
Cooking time: 50–60 minutes

French Basics

Les bases de la cuisine française

Back to basics

French cuisine is littered with terms, techniques, and *toques* (the tall white chefs' hats). It may seem all a little old-fashioned and stuffy compared to the laid-back style of the Italians or the molecular madness of the Spanish, but the French still have a lot to say in the kitchen. It's not for no reason that most culinary schools' curricula cover French cuisine. It provides students with a great foundation and understanding of cooking.

French cooking has become so embedded into the Western way of cooking that often we don't realize what we're whipping up has French origins. Take away the foreign language and what you're left with are some fundamental cooking methods. Once you understand these techniques, they can be applied and adapted to a whole variety of dishes, opening up a world of culinary possibilities.

Regardless of whether you're a beginner or a *Masterchef* contestant, knowing a few French culinary ABCs such as how to make a basic stock, *béchamel*, or salad vinaigrette will help you out in any kitchen situation.

Les Fonds/Stocks

A liquid in which meat, fish, or vegetables are simmered to extract their flavor; used as a base for soups, sauces, and stews.

The French word for "stock" is *fond*. It also means "base" or "foundation," which is a great way of describing how important stocks are in French cuisine. In fact, it's not only French dishes that benefit from a good-quality stock—the value of any dish containing stock will go up if the stock is made well.

You may think that in today's hectic world there's no time to make stock, but it doesn't take as long as you think. Ten minutes' prep and the rest is just letting it simmer gently on the stove. You'll be rewarded with something that has so much more depth and flavor than the little cubes you dissolve in water (and none of the additives).

Water, the main component of stock, costs next to nothing. You need to add your key ingredient—meat or fish bones or vegetables—plus what the French call *mirepoix* (onion, carrot, and celery) and a bouquet garni. A classic bouquet garni would be a bay leaf, peppercorns, parsley stalks, and thyme.

So, the ingredients stay practically the same regardless of what kind of stock you're making, and so does the technique. Simply pop the ingredients into a pot, simmer, and skim off the foam (the impurities and fat that rise to the surface).

There are two different types of stock in French cuisine: white (unroasted) and brown (roasted). White stock is generally used for white sauces due to its color, while brown stock has a stronger color and flavor.

Each stock uses a key component that gives it a distinct flavor:

Veal/beef
Knuckles are best as they contain collagen, which gives the stock body. The French prefer veal to beef because it makes a lighter and more delicately flavored stock (it also contains more collagen).

Poultry
Carcasses, backs, and wings of chicken or turkey (or the bird of your preference).

Fish/shellfish
Bones and heads of white fish (e.g., pollack, haddock, sole). Avoid oily fish, such as mackerel, tuna, or salmon, as they will make a cloudy stock. Shells from crustaceans (e.g., shrimp, crabs, langoustines, lobsters) also make a flavorsome stock.

Vegetable
Aromatic vegetables, such as leeks, fennel, parsnips, and celery. Mushrooms lend a meaty flavor. Avoid potatoes, sweet potatoes, pumpkins, and other starchy vegetables as they will make a cloudy stock.

Tips for a successful stock
- The golden rule for making a meat or fish stock is to start with cold water, bring it slowly to a simmer, and then keep it on a simmer throughout the cooking time.

Pourquoi? A cold start and slow heating release water-soluble proteins, which coagulate slowly into the stock and rise to the top, making it easier to skim. (A hot start produces many separate and tiny protein particles that create a murky stock, while a rolling boil makes the fat and foam come to the top and then emulsify back into the stock.)

- For all meat and fish stocks, use a combination of bones and meat with no fat.

Pourquoi? When you simmer bones, the collagen turns into gelatin and is absorbed into the stock to give it body and a silky mouthfeel. Bones don't provide much flavor, however, so that's where the meat comes into play, giving the stock taste.

Storage
Fresh meat, poultry, and vegetable stocks can be kept in an airtight container in the fridge for up to 5 days, or in the freezer for up to 3 months. Fish stock is best used the same day.

To save on storage space, simmer the stock until reduced by half and then pour into ice-cube trays and freeze. Whenever you need stock for a recipe, use a frozen cube of your own homemade stock.

WHITE (UNROASTED) STOCK
MAKES ABOUT 4½ CUPS

- 3 lb raw veal or beef knuckles/poultry carcasses, backs, and wings/fish bones and heads/shells from crustaceans
- 2 onions, quartered • 1 carrot, halved
- 1 stick of celery, halved
- 1 bouquet garni (1 bay leaf, 10 peppercorns, 5 parsley stalks, 2 sprigs of thyme)
- 6½ cups *cold* water

Place the bones in a large heavy-bottomed stockpot, cover with cold water, and bring to a boil, uncovered. Remove the bones and rinse under cold running water to remove some of the impurities.

Place the bones in a clean stockpot with the rest of the ingredients and the measured water (use a little more if needed to cover the bones). Slowly bring to a simmer, uncovered. Using a large flat ladle, remove any foam that rises to the top. Simmer for 6 hours if making veal or beef stock, 4 hours for poultry. For fish, simmer for 45 minutes to 1 hour maximum.* Keep the pan uncovered and the bones submerged in liquid at all times, skimming occasionally and topping up with warm water if necessary.

Pour through a coffee filter or a fine sieve and chill.

* *Pourquoi? It's important not to overcook fish stock as the brittle fish bones will start to dissolve calcium salts, which will cloud the stock and give it a chalky taste.*

BROWN (ROASTED) STOCK
MAKES ABOUT 4½ CUPS

- 3 lb raw veal or beef knuckles or poultry carcasses, backs, and wings*
- 2 tbsp vegetable oil (a neutral-tasting oil, not olive oil)
- 2 onions, quartered with skin left on**
- 1 carrot, halved • 1 stick of celery, halved
- 1 bouquet garni (1 bay leaf, 10 peppercorns, 5 parsley stalks, 2 sprigs of thyme)
- 6½ cups *cold* water

Preheat the oven to 400°F. Rub the bones with the oil and place them in a roasting pan with the vegetables. Roast for about an hour or until well browned.

Transfer the roasted bones and vegetables to a large heavy-bottomed stockpot. Add the aromatics and the water (use a little more if needed to cover the bones) and slowly bring to a simmer, uncovered. Using a large flat ladle, remove any foam that rises to the top. Simmer for 6 hours for veal or beef stock, 4 hours for poultry, or until the stock has a strong flavor. Keep the pan uncovered and the bones submerged in liquid at all times, skimming occasionally and topping up with warm water if necessary.

Pour through a coffee filter or a fine sieve and chill.

* *You can also use the carcasses from roast poultry and then roast the vegetables on their own at the beginning of the recipe.*

** *The onion skin enriches the color of the stock.*

Demi-glace

The old-fashioned version of *demi-glace*—equal parts roasted brown stock and *espagnole* sauce—is still seen on menus at fine-dining restaurants. You can create a modern version by simply reducing brown (roasted) stock until thick enough to coat the back of a spoon. The gelatin will thicken the sauce, so there is no need for a thickening *roux*.

VEGETABLE STOCK
MAKES ABOUT 4½ CUPS

- 1 tbsp olive oil
- 2 onions, quartered with skin left on
- 3 cloves of garlic, pounded flat
- 2 carrots, roughly chopped
- 2 sticks of celery, roughly chopped
- ½ bulb of fennel, roughly chopped
- 2 tomatoes, roughly chopped
- 8 button mushrooms, brushed or peeled and roughly chopped
- 1 bouquet garni (1 bay leaf, 10 peppercorns, 5 parsley stalks, 2 sprigs of thyme)
- ½ tsp sugar • 1 tsp salt
- 6½ cups *cold* water

Put all the ingredients, apart from the water, into a large heavy-bottomed stockpot. Fry on a high heat for 10 minutes to soften and slightly brown the vegetables. Pour in the water (add more if needed to cover the vegetables) and slowly bring to a simmer. Simmer uncovered for 30 minutes. Let cool before straining through a coffee filter or a very fine sieve.

Sauces

L'ARBRE GÉNÉALOGIQUE FRANÇAIS DES SAUCES

THE FRENCH FAMILY TREE OF SAUCES

Sauces made the French kitchen famous and their history goes back to medieval times, but it was chef Antonin Carême (1784–1833) who classified them into four categories in *L'Art de la cuisine au XIXe siècle*. These "mother sauces" are *béchamel* (creamy milk), *velouté* (white meat, fish, or vegetables), *espagnole* (brown meat), and *tomate* (tomato), each of which can be turned into another "secondary sauce" with a few extra ingredients. *Hollandaise* was created later, as the fifth and final mother sauce, and its spin-offs cover almost all forms of classic emulsions, such as *mayonnaise* and *béarnaise*.

It doesn't matter whether you roast, broil, poach, barbecue, or even serve some ingredients raw, a well-made sauce will take any meat, poultry, fish, or vegetables to the next level. A sauce shouldn't mask a dish but enhance and bring out its flavors, and, to avoid waste, sauces are a great way to make a delicious "new" meal out of leftovers.

ROUX

A *roux* is a paste used for thickening sauces that consists of equal amounts of flour and butter (or sometimes pork or duck fat). It is cooked until it no longer tastes of flour or has achieved a certain color, before the liquid for the sauce is added.

There are three different types of *roux*:

White—cooked without coloring until the flour is no longer raw. Used for *béchamel*-based sauces.

Blonde—cooked until a light golden color. Used for *velouté*-based sauces.

Brown—cooked until almost a Coca-Cola color and with a nutty taste. Used for *espagnole*-based sauces.

SAUCE BÉCHAMEL

SERVES 4–6

A milk sauce thickened with a white *roux* and seasoned with onion, clove, and bay leaf. The easiest of the mother sauces, *béchamel* is a favorite for smothering almost anything and making it comforting—see the recipes for *Gratin au poisson fumé* (page 50) and *Endives au jambon* (page 159).

- **2 tbsp butter • ¼ cup all-purpose flour**
- **2 cups milk, lukewarm**
- **¼ onion, skin removed • 1 clove • 1 bay leaf**
- **a pinch of nutmeg • salt and white pepper**

Over a medium heat, melt the butter in a large pan and add the flour. Using a wooden spoon, beat hard to a smooth paste *(roux)*. Take off the heat.

Start adding the milk to the *roux* by beating in about 2 tablespoons, then repeat until you have incorporated about a quarter of the milk. Switch to a whisk and gradually incorporate the rest of the milk.

Place the pan back over a medium heat and simmer with the onion, clove, and bay leaf for 10 minutes. Whisk frequently to ensure that none of the sauce burns on the bottom of the pan. If the sauce becomes too thick (it should have the consistency of custard or a thick tomato sauce), whisk in a little more milk.

Remove the onion, clove, and bay leaf, then add the nutmeg and season with salt and white pepper (black pepper is fine if you don't mind the speckles).

Mornay (cheese) sauce: before seasoning at the end, add 1¾ cups grated Gruyère or mature Comté cheese (or a strong hard cheese like Cheddar or Parmesan).

Creamy mustard sauce: stir in a generous tablespoon of grainy mustard before seasoning at the end.

Caper and parsley sauce: add 2 tablespoons chopped capers and a handful of chopped parsley before seasoning at the end.

VELOUTÉ SAUCES

These are made with a blonde *roux* as for a *béchamel* except that the milk is replaced by white (unroasted) stock or vegetable stock.

Velouté sauces are not served on their own but used as a base for a wide range of other sauces. Different stocks will influence the end result (vegetable stock making the lightest of sauces), and you can add chopped button mushrooms, fresh herbs such as tarragon and dill, or spices like paprika. Use your taste buds and get creative!

Sauce Bercy (below) is a classic *velouté* sauce. For examples of other *velouté* sauces in action, see *Poulet aux champignons avec une sauce au vin blanc* (page 187) and *Asperges à la parisienne* (page 156).

SAUCE BERCY
SERVES 4

Traditionally made with a fish *velouté* (blonde *roux* plus fish stock) with shallots, butter, and white wine but no cream. A perfect match for seafood.

For the velouté *sauce:* 2 tbsp butter
• ¼ cup all-purpose flour • 1¾ cups fish stock
• 2 shallots, finely chopped

• 4 tbsp butter • ½ cup dry white wine
• salt • a few drops of lemon juice
• a handful of chopped parsley

TO MAKE THE *VELOUTÉ* SAUCE: Melt the butter in a large pot over a medium heat and add the flour. Using a wooden spoon, beat hard until you have a smooth paste *(roux)*. Continue to beat until the *roux* begins to have a light golden color. Take off the heat.

Start adding the stock to the *roux* by beating in about 2 tablespoons, then repeat until you have incorporated about a quarter of the stock. Switch to a whisk and gradually incorporate the rest of the stock.

Place the pot back over a medium heat and simmer for 15–20 minutes. Whisk frequently to ensure that none of the sauce burns on the bottom of the pan. If the sauce becomes too thick (it should have the consistency of custard or a thick tomato sauce), whisk in a little more stock. Remove from the heat.

To finish, cook the shallots with 2 tablespoons of butter in a large frying pan until translucent. Add

the wine and reduce for 2 minutes before pouring in the *velouté* sauce. Simmer for 5 minutes. Season with salt and lemon juice. Before serving, swirl in the remaining butter and add the chopped parsley.

SAUCE ESPAGNOLE
SERVES 4

A classic in French cuisine, and the last time I counted I found over twenty different offspring. No wonder, when it's so versatile.

The classic *sauce espagnole* is reduced for several hours. This is my modern shortcut version, which can be served as it comes with roasted, broiled, or poached meat, or you can add extra ingredients* to make a fine accompaniment to almost any dish.

• 1 oz lardons or cubes of smoked bacon**
• 1 onion, finely chopped
• 1 carrot, finely chopped
• 1 stick of celery, finely chopped
• 2 tbsp butter • ¼ cup all-purpose flour
• 2 cups veal or beef stock, lukewarm
• 1 tbsp tomato paste
• 1 bouquet garni (1 bay leaf, 10 peppercorns, 5 parsley stalks, 2 sprigs of thyme)

Over a medium heat, fry the lardons and vegetables until golden. Remove with a slotted spoon, trying to keep as much of the fat as possible in the pan. Melt the butter in the pan, sprinkle in the flour, and stir constantly until it turns almost a Coca-Cola color (this is a brown *roux*). Reduce the heat to low and slowly pour in the warm stock while whisking energetically. Once the stock is incorporated, add the tomato paste and whisk until dissolved. Pop the fried vegetables and lardons back into the pan, add the bouquet garni, and simmer gently for 15 minutes. Pour through a sieve (to remove the vegetables, lardons, bouquet garni, and any other bits) to make a silky-smooth sauce. Taste for seasoning.***

* See the recipes for Oeufs en meurette (page 26), and Saucisse et purée de pomme de terre avec une sauce diable (page 69).

** If you prefer not to use pork, replace the lardons with 1 tablespoon butter.

*** If you like, stir in 2–3 tablespoons crème fraîche just before tasting for seasoning.

TOMATO SAUCES

These no-fuss sauces are good back-up recipes. They can be prepared in advance and even frozen.

ESCOFFIER'S TOMATO SAUCE
SERVES 4–6

You may think that the Italians have mastered the art of tomato sauces but Escoffier's* is a pretty mean sauce too. The addition of lardons and veal stock gives it a deep, meaty-rich flavor, and you can add a dash of heavy cream or 2 tablespoons of butter before serving if you wish.

This is my adaptation of Escoffier's classic recipe.

- 2 tbsp butter
- 1 clove of garlic, crushed to a paste
- 1¾ oz lardons or cubes of smoked bacon
- 1 carrot, chopped into medium dice
- 1 onion, finely chopped
- ¼ cup all-purpose flour
- 2 cups veal or beef stock, lukewarm
- 2 lb tomatoes, roughly chopped
- a pinch of sugar, or to taste • salt and pepper

Melt the butter in a large pan. Add the garlic, lardons, carrot, and onion and sweat on a medium heat for 10 minutes or until the vegetables are soft and some of the fat from the lardons has melted. Sprinkle in the flour and cook for another couple of minutes, then whisk continuously while slowly pouring in the stock.

Add the tomatoes and simmer, covered, for an hour or until they have broken down completely.

Whizz the sauce in a blender until smooth. Season to taste with the sugar, salt, and pepper.

Auguste Escoffier (1846–1935) modernized and popularized French cooking as we know it today. In 1903 he published Le Guide culinaire, *which is still regarded as a major reference work for professional cooks, both for recipes and kitchen management. Drawing on his experience in the French army, Escoffier organized the kitchen team by hierarchy of authority, responsibility, and function, with each individual delegated a specific task. This system is still used throughout the restaurant world today.*

MODERN TOMATO SAUCE (VEGAN)
SERVES 2–3

- 1 onion, finely chopped
- 1 carrot, finely chopped
- 1 stick of celery, finely chopped
- 1 clove of garlic, crushed to a paste
- 2 tbsp olive oil
- one 16-oz can tomatoes, chopped
- a pinch of sugar • salt and pepper

Sweat the onion, carrot, celery, and garlic with the olive oil for 10 minutes or until tender. Add the chopped tomatoes and simmer, covered, for an hour.

Whizz the sauce in a blender until smooth. Season with the sugar, salt, and pepper.

SAUCES AU BEURRE
BUTTER SAUCES

These simple sauces are probably the quickest way to add extra flavor to fish (see *Poisson meunière* on page 180), meat, poultry, and vegetables. There's not much to them, apart from melting a little butter.

BEURRE BLANC
SERVES 2–3

- 1 shallot, finely chopped
- 6 tbsp dry white wine
- 4 tbsp white wine vinegar
- 4 tbsp heavy cream
- 6½ tbsp butter, cubed
- salt • a pinch of cayenne pepper

Simmer the shallot, wine, and vinegar in a pan until reduced to 1 tablespoon. Remove the pan from the heat and whisk in the cream followed by a cube of butter at a time. Make sure to whisk energetically. If the butter isn't melting, put the pan back on a low heat. Once all the butter is incorporated, season with salt and a little cayenne. Serve immediately.

Chopped herbs, such as mint, parsley, basil or tarragon, make a nice addition.

BEURRE NOISETTE
SERVES 2

• 6½ tbsp butter, cubed
• 1 tbsp chopped parsley

Put the butter into a large pan and place on a medium heat. Cook until the butter has become a nutty brown color, then remove from the heat and add the parsley. Serve immediately.

BEURRE AU CITRON
SERVES 2

• juice of 1 lemon • 4 tbsp dry white wine
• 6½ tbsp butter, cubed • salt

Simmer the lemon juice and wine in a pan until reduced to 1 tablespoon. Remove the pan from the heat and whisk in the butter a cube at a time. Make sure to whisk energetically. If the butter isn't melting, put the pan back on a low heat. Once all the butter is incorporated, season with a little salt. Serve immediately.

LES ÉMULSIONS
DRESSINGS

These use liquids that don't normally bind together easily. They are combined by rapid mixing to make them smooth, and are renowned for being the trickiest of sauces to make. With my recipes and a few tips and tricks, though, they should be a doddle.

HOLLANDAISE
SERVES 2–3

Although the name suggests Dutch origins, historians claim that *sauce hollandaise* was a French invention most likely dating from the mid-eighteenth century. Hollandaise sauce and asparagus is like mint and peas—a match made in heaven—but hollandaise can be served with other vegetables too (it's particularly nice with long-stemmed purple broccoli that can be dipped into the sauce).

• 3 egg yolks, at room temperature
• ¾ cup plus 2 tbsp butter, melted and still warm
• juice of ½ lemon • salt and pepper

Place a large heatproof bowl over a pot of simmering water. Put the egg yolks into the bowl and whisk them at the same time as adding the melted warm butter, drop by drop. Whisk constantly* until the sauce has the consistency of thick cream. Take off the heat, add the lemon juice, and season with salt and pepper. Use immediately.

* Make sure to whisk constantly and vigorously as this helps to disperse the water and oil droplets evenly, and so stop the sauce separating.

Sauce Béarnaise: Place 6 tablespoons each dry white wine and white wine vinegar in a pan with 10 peppercorns and a finely chopped shallot. Simmer until reduced by half. Strain and leave to cool for a couple of minutes (it should be lukewarm, not boiling), then whisk into the finished hollandaise sauce followed by 2 tablespoons chopped tarragon. (If you replace the tarragon with mint, you will have a sauce paloise, which is great with lamb and mutton.)

Sauce Maltaise: Simmer 7 tablespoons orange juice in a pan until reduced to about 2 tablespoons. Fold into the finished hollandaise sauce with the finely grated zest of 1 orange. Check for seasoning.

Sauce Mousseline: Whisk 1 egg white to soft peaks and fold into the finished hollandaise sauce. Check for seasoning.

MAYONNAISE
SERVES 2–3

• 3 egg yolks, at room temperature
• ¾–1 cup sunflower or vegetable oil*
• a few drops of white wine vinegar
or lemon juice • salt

Place the egg yolks in a large glass or stainless-steel bowl set on a damp tea towel (this will stop the bowl from slipping). Start by whisking the egg yolks a little, then add the oil drop by drop until the eggs begin to thicken and become pale in color.

Continue by drizzling the oil into the mix until you have achieved the consistency you like. Add a few drops of white wine vinegar or lemon juice and season with salt.

* *If you would like your mayonnaise to have the peppery taste of olive oil, switch to an extra virgin olive oil when the mixture has become thick and pale in color. I find using only olive oil gives the mayonnaise a bitter taste.*

Chopped fresh herbs, such as parsley, dill, tarragon, or basil, make a great addition to mayonnaise.

If you like a little heat, why not try adding a little wasabi, harissa, or sweet chile sauce?

Sauce Tartare: Mix 1 tablespoon each chopped capers, cornichons, parsley, tarragon, and chervil into the mayonnaise.

Sauce Cocktail: Mix 1 tablespoon tomato ketchup into the mayonnaise with 1 teaspoon each Cognac and Worcestershire sauce and a dash of Tabasco or a pinch of cayenne pepper.

VINAIGRETTE

MAKES ENOUGH FOR A
GREEN SALAD TO SERVE 4–6

Vinaigrette wasn't always associated with salad dressings. From the late-eighteenth century until the middle of the nineteenth, it was the name given to a small box made of gold, mother-of-pearl, or ivory. Fashionable ladies of the time wore the box on a necklace and inside they kept a small sponge soaked in aromatic vinegar. The sponge was used to dab foreheads and temples when the ladies felt flushed.

I think a much better way of handling hot flushes is to eat a perfectly dressed fresh green salad. The French know how to dress, both in fashion and salad terms. They keep it simple and classic.

A ratio of 3 parts oil to 1 part acid is a general rule of thumb when making vinaigrette, but at the end of the day your personal taste can always make it a little more or less acidic.

Once you know the basics, feel free to add different types of mustard to your vinaigrette, or chopped herbs, shallots, or chile. For other ideas, see the recipe for *Salade de carottes râpées et rémoulade de céleri-rave et pommes* (page 110).

- 6 tbsp oil*
- 2 tbsp vinegar or lemon juice
- 1 tsp salt
- a generous pinch of sugar

Use an empty clean jar to shake the oil and vinegar, or whisk them together in a bowl, making sure they blend together well. Season with the salt and sugar. Try the dressing by dipping in a salad leaf and tasting, then adjust the seasoning to your liking if necessary. As long as it doesn't contain herbs, vinaigrette will keep in an airtight container in a cool cupboard for months, although it will need to be stirred or shaken (if kept in a jar) before using.

* *Vegetable or sunflower oil will give the dressing a delicate taste, whereas extra virgin olive oil is more robust in flavor. I find a combination of both works well. You can also experiment with other oils that have a distinctive taste, such as hazelnut, pistachio, and pumpkin.*

How to make your own vinegar

If you're like me and sometimes end up with leftover wine and don't know what to do with it, you could have a go at making your own vinegar (although you can freeze wine in an ice-cube tray and use it for cooking later). Homemade vinegar is easy and tends to have a more complex flavor than store-bought varieties.

You will need equal amounts of red wine* and organic cider vinegar (or live vinegar).** Stir them together and pour into a clean large container with a loose-fitting lid, making sure there's enough room for air to circulate. Cover with a piece of cheesecloth and then the lid and store in a cool, dark place for 1 week.

Remove the lid and cheesecloth and take a sniff—it should have a dominate smell and taste of vinegar with a light aroma of wine. It can be used at this stage, but it will develop more flavor if left for another week. When you need vinegar for kitchen use, pour some off and then top up the base with new wine. The vinegar will continue to develop more flavor the longer you leave it and can be kept in a dark cupboard for six months.

* *White wine or Champagne can be used instead of red wine.*

** *Pourquoi? Organic cider vinegar contains live bacteria that turn the wine into vinegar.*

Crème pâtissière

PASTRY CREAM
MAKES ABOUT 3 CUPS

Crème pâtissière (pastry cream) might not sound like the most exciting French dessert recipe but it is a great one to know.

Once you have the hang of making it, there'll be no stopping you. Fill *éclairs, millefeuilles,* tarts, cakes, doughnuts, or trifles, or fold in some whipped cream to make a simple mousse or, as the French call it, a *crème Madame.* The possibilities are endless. And then there are also countless flavors: vanilla, chocolate, coffee, orange, cinnamon. You could probably incorporate pastry cream into any dessert, it's that versatile. It can also be made in advance and kept in the fridge for 2–3 days. *Café Gourmande* (page 212) is a great example of the versatility of *crème pâtissière.* All you have to do is make one quantity of the basic recipe and with a couple of extra ingredients you can then create three mini desserts: strawberry and vanilla tartlets, orange mousse, and crème de cassis trifle. Ssssssshhhhh, don't tell anyone how simple it is, though—your friends will be less impressed.

- 6 egg yolks
- ½ cup superfine sugar
- ⅓ cup cornstarch • 1 vanilla pod*
- 2 cups milk

Whisk the egg yolks with the sugar until light and thick, then whisk in the cornstarch.

Split the vanilla pod in half and scrape out the grains, using the back of a knife. Add the vanilla pod and grains (or your choice of flavoring) to the milk. Bring the milk to a boil and switch off the heat. Remove the vanilla pod and pour the milk in a slow stream onto the egg mixture, whisking vigorously all the time.

Return the mixture to a clean pot and continuously whisk over a medium heat. Make sure to scrape the sides and the bottom, otherwise it will burn. The cream will start to thicken. Once it releases a bubble or two, take it off the heat.

Pour onto a tray lined with plastic wrap. Cover with plastic wrap (pat the plastic wrap so it sticks directly onto the cream) and refrigerate for at least an hour before using.

* Instead of a vanilla pod, try these other flavors:

Chocolate: 2 heaped tablespoons unsweetened cocoa powder

Coffee: 2 teaspoons instant coffee powder

Mocha: 2 teaspoons instant coffee powder, 1 heaped tablespoon unsweetened cocoa powder

Citrus: zest of 1 orange, lemon, or lime or a combination of all three

Lavender: 1 teaspoon dried lavender (remove from the infused milk before incorporating with the eggs)

Tea: 2 heaped tablespoons Earl Grey, green, or matcha tea (remove tea leaves from the infused milk before incorporating with the eggs)

Spices: try cinnamon, ginger, tonka bean, nutmeg, chile (works particularly well with chocolate)

PREPARATION TIME: 20 MINUTES RESTING TIME: 1 HOUR
COOKING TIME: 20 MINUTES

Cook's Notes

Unless otherwise stated, I've used the following ingredients in the recipes:

- *coarse sea salt*
- *freshly ground black pepper*
- *freshly grated nutmeg*
- *whole milk*
- *unsalted butter*
- *superfine sugar*
- *medium-sized fruits and vegetables*
- *large eggs*
- *bouquet garni: 1 bay leaf, 10 peppercorns, 5 parsley stalks, 2 sprigs of thyme*

Spoon measures are level unless otherwise stated

Fahrenheit temperatures are given for conventional ovens. For convection ovens reduce the temperature by 25–50°F, or according to manufacturer's instructions. For other ovens, see the conversion chart on the opposite page.

Weights

7.5 g	¼ oz	85 g	3 oz	340 g	12 oz	1.1 kg	2½ lb
15 g	½ oz	100 g	3½ oz	370 g	13 oz	1.4 kg	3 lb
20 g	¾ oz	115 g	4 oz	400 g	14 oz	1.5 kg	3½ lb
30 g	1 oz	140 g	5 oz	425 g	15 oz	1.8 kg	4 lb
35 g	1¼ oz	170 g	6 oz	455 g	1 lb	2 kg	4½ lb
40 g	1½ oz	200 g	7 oz	565 g	1¼ lb	2.3 kg	5 lb
50 g	1¾ oz	225 g	8 oz	680 g	1½ lb	2.7 kg	6 lb
55 g	2 oz	255 g	9 oz	795 g	1¾ lb	3.1 kg	7 lb
65 g	2¼ oz	285 g	10 oz	905 g	2 lb	3.6 kg	8 lb
70 g	2½ oz	310 g	11 oz	1 kg	2 lb 3 oz	4.5 kg	10 lb

Oven Temperatures

Very cool	110°C	225°F	Gas ¼
Very cool	130°C	250°F	Gas ½
Cool	140°C	275°F	Gas 1
Slow	150°C	300°F	Gas 2
Moderately slow	160°C	325°F	Gas 3
Moderate	180°C	350°F	Gas 4
Moderately hot	190°C	375°F	Gas 5
Hot	200°C	400°F	Gas 6
Very hot	220°C	425°F	Gas 7
Very hot	230°C	450°F	Gas 8
Hottest	240°C	475°F	Gas 9

My Paris addresses

It's impossible to list all the amazing foodie places in Paris, so I've just popped my regulars down.

Le Bal café

It's not often you find two women running a restaurant in Paris and even more unusual to find two Englishwomen. They cook up a storm with their English dishes with a French twist. It's not just the Brit expats like me who are loving their cooking; the French are too.

6 impasse de la Défense
75018 Paris

Le Baratin

Off a little side street in Paris's second Chinatown, Belleville, you'll find this restaurant serving simple, tasty French food and a great selection of wines.

3 rue Jouye Rouve
75020 Paris

Le Baron rouge

After all that hard work doing the food shopping, I like to pop into this charming wine bar which is just off marché d'Aligre. At the weekend they serve oysters in addition to a great plate of charcuterie or cheese.

1 rue Théophile Roussel
75012 Paris

Bob's juice bar

When I need a break from French food, I like to pop by Bob's for a juice and a healthful salad.

15 rue Lucien Sampaix
75010 Paris

www.bobsjuicebar.com

Boucherie Leclerc

My local butchers, who are always serving with a smile and happy to give me some advice on how to cook the meat perfectly.

53 rue Meaux
75019 Paris

Café Chéri(e)

My local. Not typically Parisian, being right in the heart of the second Chinatown in Paris, but it makes for interesting people-watching.

44 Boulevard de la Villette
75019 Paris

Le Chateaubriand

Diners put their appetites into Chef Inaki Aizpitarte's very capable hands with his evening fixed menu. A little difficult to get a reservation but you can turn up before 9 p.m. and wait at the bar for a table to become available.

129 avenue Parmentier
75011 Paris

La Cocotte

Cute culinary store selling their own cooking accessories (tea towels) and a small selection of well-chosen cookbooks.

5 rue Paul Bert
75011 Paris

www.lacocotte.net

G. Detou

If you're looking for 5kg bags of blanched almonds or a 10kg bag of chocolate buttons, then this is a place for you. Stocked with a huge range of French delicacies (not all in large bags). I guarantee it'll be hard to walk out the door empty handed.

58 rue Tiquetonne
75002 Paris

Du pain et des idées

www.dupainetdesidees.com

They do great little rolls with different fillings (*lardons*, cheese, sundried tomatoes, figs . . .) and their pain des amis is very good too.

34 rue Yves Toudic
75010 Paris

Gontran Cherrier

www.gontrancherrierboulanger.com

The charming French baker from pages 112–15.

22 rue Caulaincourt
75018 Paris

Le Grain du riz

If you're fed up with the typical French service, this tiny Vietnamese restaurant (virtually the size of a rice grain) serves genuine delicious Vietnamese food with a warm, friendly smile.

49 rue Godefroy Cavaignac
75011 Paris

Ma cave en ville

My local wine dealer. A great selection of wine with a lot of hard-to-find, organic and natural wines.

105 rue Belleville
75019 Paris

Marché d'Aligre

Each neighbourhood will have a fresh produce market once or twice a week (apart from Mondays). The marché d'Aligre is open Tuesday–Sunday mornings. The selection is large, with covered and open-air areas, plus there are some great North African grocery stores.

Rue d'aligre
75012 Paris

Mora

www.mora.fr

This store is a treasure trove for any budding chef. A little pricey, but all the products sold in the store are of good quality. In the same street there are a few other chef stores: A. Simon and Bovida.

13 rue Montmartre
75001 Paris

À la petite fabrique du chocolat

This little chocolate shop was just around the corner from my first apartment in Paris, which wasn't a very good thing. My favourite is their dark chocolate praline bar. *C'est tellement terrible* (it's so bad, delicious) that I even managed to eat a whole bar in one sitting.

12 rue Saint-Sabin
75011 Paris

Septime

Young chef Bertrand Grébaut won a grant from Evian-Badoit to open up his restaurant and realize his dream of making *haute cuisine* accessible to everyone. I love his modern take on French food using the best seasonal ingredients.

80 rue Charonne
75011 Paris

For more of my favourites, see

http://www.rachelkhoo.com/my-favourite-places-in-paris

Index

Bold numbers indicate photos.

Acknowledgments

This book would have never happened if my editor, Lindsey Evans, hadn't responded to my "cold-call" e-mail and given thirty minutes of her time for me to pitch my "Little Paris Kitchen" cookbook idea (a special thank you to Sarah Canet at Spoon PR for giving me her e-mail address). Lindsey, thanks for taking a chance on me and supporting me in writing my French classics.

Thanks also to—

John Hamilton: your enthusiasm and vision have made this book something special.

David Loftus: for being as excited as me about doing this book and of course for making the food (and me) look stunning.

The Penguin team: *merci à tous* for your devotion and eagerness to make this book a success.

Elodie Rambaud: your "cute" touches have made this book beautiful.

Frankie Unsworth: you're the best culinary assistant in the world and the best foodie partner in crime, too!

Lizzy Kremer and the team at David Higham: thanks for always being on call.

Un grand merci to all of my guests who came for lunch at La petite cuisine à Paris. And to all of those who tried to come, I wish I could have had you all over for lunch.

Lana and Misha Citron: without you guys, I would have never made it onto the Eurostar with all my luggage when I moved to Paris. Lana, your encouragement and faith in me has helped me enormously over the years.

Benjamin Rurka: thanks for always believing that I'll make it.

Kami, Loïs, Claire et Bertrand Soleil: *merci mille fois* for making me feel at home and showing me the Parisian way of life when I first moved here.

Andrea Wainer: *merci* for giving me my first culinary job in Paris and opening up a whole world of new opportunities.

My friends (or rather, my recipe guinea pigs!): thanks for being up for eating my experiments (even if they weren't always that delicious).

Many thanks to Astier de Villatte (www.astierdevillatte.com) and to Le Creuset (www.lecreuset.fr) for lovely props.

And finally, my family, who have been there through thick and thin. Without your love and support, I wouldn't be where I am now.

Fin

LES FEUILLES DE LAURIER

LE THON

LES AMANDES

LE CAHIER

LA VAISSELLE

LE FENOUIL

LE FOUR

L'HUITRE

LES CHANTERELLES

LA COCOTTE

LA CARAFE D'EAU

LE POULET

LE PASTIS

LES FROMAGES

LE COCKTAIL

LE TIRE BOUCHON

LES POMMES DE TERRE

LE CÈPE

LE BOL

LES POIVRONS

LE GÂTEAU

LA RHUBARBE

LA SALADE

L'ORANGE

LE SUCRE

LA LAVANDE

LE SANDWICH

LE MOULIN À POIVRE

LES PIMENTS

LA FARINE

LA POIRE

LES ALLUMETTES

LE PANIER

LE ROMARIN

LE THÉ

LA MENTHE

LE LAIT

UNE PLANCHE À DÉCOUPER

LE ROULEAU À PÂTISSERIE

LES ABEILLES

LE SAC À DOS

LA BAGUETTE

LES SERVIETTES

LES OIGNONS FRAIS

L'HUILE D'OLIVE

L'ARBRE

LE CITRON

LE SAUCISSON